As all things, for Whitey...
who I was lucky enough to have as my husband.

ACCLAIM FOR MARILYN

"Love, love, love the interview…I have had many interviews done…I simply love this one. The facts, only the facts, and you got them right. Thank you." — Carol Connors, singer & two-time Oscar-nominated songwriter.

"What a FABULOUS article — BRAVO TO YOU! It's just fabulous. And Dorothy Dale Kloss is thrilled!" — Ken Prescott, actor, singer, dancer, producer.

"You did a great job on the story and I am thrilled. I have received a lot of comments about it so you are well read! Again, my thanks for your thoughtfulness and talent as a journalist." — Gloria Greer, journalist, TV host & Producer, KVCR-TV & Time Warner Cable.

"Well, Marilyn Mitchell, this is the greatest article ever written about me. I'm moved to tears. You're the best. It's hard for the person being interviewed to get the essence of who they are and what they're about…but you got it. This has certainly brightened my day and how nice it was you chose me. You are awesome! Thank you." — Pattie Daly Caruso, TV host & Producer, KPSP Local 2.

"I wanted to write you how much I enjoyed the article you wrote on Pattie Daly Caruso. I thought you captured the true essence of our dear friend. You have a wonderful way with words. If you didn't know Pattie, you'd want to after reading it. I look forward to more of your articles." — Ginny Haenel.

"Thanks, Marilyn. It's terrific. I can't thank you enough for the article and the wonderful way you took the information and wove it into an interesting story. You made me look good and I really appreciate that. I'm going to send it to my family in Illinois right now." — Tom Dreesen

"Read your article about Frankie Randall. You have a certain flair in your style of writing I like. It's newsy with detail. That's what makes it interesting. You have a fan in me." — Lynne Friedman Vaughan, Author.

"Your stories are always good!" — Gary Willhide, editor, Desert Entertainer Magazine.

"I've heard about so many Sinatra sightings through the years, but none so charming as yours." — Allene Arthur, columnist, the Desert Sun.

"Writing this short note to thank you very much for the great article you did on me." — Trini Lopez.

"I still treasure the beautiful story you wrote about me." — Rhonda Fleming.

"Wanted you to know how much I enjoyed reading your article." — Melinda Read, TV host & Producer, Time Warner Cable.

"What a great article! You told a compelling story about what the Palm Springs Walk of Stars is all about. Congratulations!" — Allan Bregman, producer PSWOS board member

"A million thank yous for the wonderful story! We sent it to CBS." — Dan McGrath, on-air radio personality, EZ-103.1 FM.

"Great Job! I love the article. Thank you." — Denise DuBarry Hay, Actress, Producer, Entrepreneur.

Walking With The Stars
© 2011 Marilyn Mitchell. All Rights Reserved.

No part of this book may be reproduced in any form or by any means, electronic, mechanical, digital, photocopying or recording, except for the inclusion in a review, without permission in writing from the publisher.

While all information in this book was derived firsthand from interviews with each living star recipient, all reasonable steps have been taken to ensure any additional information is accurate and up-to-date at time of publication. Neither the author nor BearManor Media shall be responsible for any factual errors or misinformation contained herein. All photos have been used with permission, either given by the star, their representative, or taken by the author.

Published in the USA by:
BearManor Media
PO Box 1129
Duncan, Oklahoma 73534-1129
www.bearmanormedia.com

ISBN 978-1-59393-661-7

Printed in the United States of America.
Book design by Brian Pearce | Red Jacket Press.

WALKING
WITH
THE
STARS

MARILYN MITCHELL

TABLE OF CONTENTS

FOREWORD.................................... 9
A STAR IS BORN............................. 13
DANE ANDREW................................ 17
WILLIAM ASHER.............................. 21
TED BACINO................................. 25
CARROLL BAKER.............................. 29
KAYE BALLARD............................... 33
RONA BARRETT............................... 37
CLIFF BOLE................................. 41
PATTIE DALY CARUSO......................... 45
CAROL CHANNING............................. 49
CAROL CONNORS.............................. 55
MICHAEL DANTE.............................. 59
KAL DAVID & LAURI BONO..................... 63
TOM DREESEN................................ 67
JOEY ENGLISH............................... 71
SONNY EVARO & FAMILY....................... 75
RHONDA FLEMING............................. 79
RUTH GIBSON................................ 83
BUDDY GRECO & LEZLIE ANDERS................ 87
GLORIA GREER............................... 91
MEL HABER.................................. 95
MONTY HALL................................. 99

DENISE DuBARRY HAY	103
HERB JEFFRIES	107
JACK JONES	111
DOROTHY DALE KLOSS	115
RUTA LEE	119
RICH LITTLE	123
TRINI LOPEZ	127
ANITA MALTIN	131
BILL MARX	135
DAN McGRATH	139
GORDON "WHITEY" MITCHELL	143
GRACE & PHIL MOODY	151
THE NEW CHRISTY MINSTRELS AND RANDY SPARKS	155
FRANKIE RANDALL	159
MELINDA READ	163
DEBBIE REYNOLDS	167
DEL SHORES	171
BARBARA SINATRA	175
FRANK SINATRA	179
KEELY SMITH	183
SUSAN STAFFORD	187
CONNIE STEVENS	191
JERRY VALE	195
MAMIE VAN DOREN	199
DICK VAN PATTEN	203
ADAM WEST	207
DAN WESTFALL	211

FOREWORD

While some of the biggest names in show business, such as Frank Sinatra, Marilyn Monroe, Bob Hope, Carol Channing, Sophia Loren and many other mega-celebrities, are honored on the glamorous Walk of Stars, there may be a few whose star would generate a full-fledged "who's that?" But if you learned the story of the person behind the name, you can bet they've left their indelible imprint, contributed greatly to the entertainment world or made a difference in the community. Not to mention the family and friends they held dear who reverently stood up on that star day, offering a touching, sometimes tearful tribute in their behalf.

With the exception of Frank Sinatra and my dear, late husband, Gordon "Whitey" Mitchell, I have written only about those star recipients who are still with us as of now.

It's been a huge pleasure interviewing and learning about the lives and accomplishments of these remarkable star recipients. I hope you'll feel the same way.

Marilyn Mitchell
(Who's that?)

"Keep your eyes on the stars, and your feet on the ground."
Theodore Roosevelt

"That way, you'll be able to walk all over these people."
Marilyn Mitchell

Bob Alexander, president of the PSWOS.

A STAR IS BORN

It was in 1991 when producer and restaurant/hotel manager Gerhard Frenzel and entrepreneur Barbara Foster-Henderson approached the city with the idea to start the Palm Springs Walk of Stars in conjunction with the *Palm Springs Follies* premiere. The late former actor/singer/songwriter/congressman Sonny Bono was mayor then and, since Palm Springs had already been discovered by Hollywood's movie crowd, it seemed like a natural. Frenzel and Henderson easily won the city's approval, held a fundraiser, and garnered enough money to dedicate five stars. The late Johnny Grant, chairman of the Hollywood Walk of Fame and Honorary Mayor of Hollywood, participated in the dedications.

"Gerhard was chairman for twelve years and when he retired, he asked me to take over," says Bob Alexander, president of the PSWOS since 2002. Today, there is a twelve-member board, which meets once a month. Three board members, past and present, have stars themselves: Susan Stafford, Janie Hughes, and my late husband, musician/screenwriter Gordon Whitey Mitchell. Other board members are: Marilyn Ball, Bill Beck, Kathleen Bennett, John Bolivar, Allan Bregman, Lew DaSilva, Charles Dunn, Clancy Grass and Herb Gronauer.

"We're a 501-C3 public benefit foundation," says Alexander. "We provide scholarships to students of the arts and other worthy categories. We have a five-year contract with the city granting us authorization to conduct dedications on the public walkways."

Here's what it takes to get a star: You must have contributed greatly in your respective category and have become prominent by distinguishing yourself as an actor, writer, director, producer, musician, or other artistic category in the entertainment field. Other categories are civic leader, pioneer, author, humanitarian, sports star, and Congressional Medal of Honor awardee. You can be nominated by anyone or by a group.

There are three nomination forms; a dedication criteria, an application completed in the sponsor's own words, and a waiver of donor. The cost is $10,000, which includes perpetual cleaning and repainting once a year. A celebration after-party is funded separately by the sponsor. The star recipient receives a proclamation from the mayor, formally pronouncing that day to be his/her day. Several other City Council members, government officials, and board members present plaques, including a framed star replica.

Depending on availability, the recipient can select his/her location, which may have special meaning. A perfect example is the late Leon Greenberg, former owner of LG's Steakhouse, whose star sits at the restaurant's front door. "The first star I presided over as president," Bob recalls, "was for Leon Greenberg. On the day preceding the ceremony, I saw the name I ordered imprinted on the star as 'Greenburg,' not 'Greenberg.' I persuaded the sandblaster to fly back from out of town to make a new star overnight. It cost $2,500 to make the correction!"

Oscar-winner Sophia Loren on her star day.

I asked Bob about some of the more unusual dedications: "We've had a number of weird and wonderful approaches," he acknowledged. "A few came in a fire truck, one in a horse & buggy, antique cars, a farm tractor, some simply walking onto the scene wearing a tuxedo, and one or two in outrageous costumes. The late Hollywood Western actor Chris Alcaide liked his star so much he ordered a duplicate for his tombstone." I myself had an electrifying moment when, on Kathy Griffin's star day, I turned a corner and bumped smack into Barry Manilow, Carol Channing and Suzanne Somers, who all showed up to surprise her!

Basically functioning as a stage manager, Kevin Halladay takes care of the physical set-up, the podium, red carpet, chairs, taping off the area, notifying the police department for crowd control, and other behind-the-scenes duties. John Bolivar, handling sound, has his own challenges.

He makes sure no one trips over his wires and oftentimes can't easily find the city's power source. Always on hand in full costume, and to the crowd's delight, is Charlie Chaplin look-alike and Hollywood Ambassador Audrey Ruttan.

Bob says another challenge is maintaining a walkway for foot traffic, while providing access to the shops they're semi-blocking. "The stores are generally happy because we attract a crowd, many of whom become customers. But the real challenge these days is the economy. Let's face it, while our cause is great, it doesn't exactly tug at your heartstrings in the same way as heart disease or cancer."

There are presently 335 stars immortalized on the PSWOS and Alexander hopes to someday boast 1,000. His only regret is that he wasn't there to see Sophia Loren. A new project of which he's proud is an audio tour book, allowing walking visitors to listen on their cell phones to a 30-second biography of their favorite stars.

Some notables the board is working on for near-future dedications are actress Lindsay Wagner, primatologist Dr. Jane Goodall, and racing cyclist Lance Armstrong. A group of fans are gathering funds for actress Brigitte Nielsen and fans recently honored the late screen legend Loretta Young. If you'd like to nominate someone for a star, call the office at 760-416-5811.

Robert Alexander is a producer, concert and record promoter who co-produced 150 Sinatra, My Way *shows and two pilots, which aired on CBS-TV. He founded the Motion Picture Hall of Fame, which produced* Latin Music Legends *and* Entertainment Las Vegas Style, *aired on PBS.*

Dane Andrew on star day with Rascal, the world's ugliest dog.

THIS IS NO SHAGGY DOG STORY
DANE ANDREW

STAR #284
DEDICATED MAY 5, 2007
200 S. PALM CANYON DR.

Dane Andrew got a jump on show business early in his hometown of Sunnyvale, California, when, by age eleven, he had already made several television appearances with his first best friend, Chi-Chi, who was then the "World's Ugliest Dog!"

While in school, Dane became a cablecaster, broadcasting live news and information for Cable TV-3 and CCN-TV in the San Francisco area. It all started one life-changing day when Dane was approached on campus by the host of a local television show, who was desperately seeking a cameraman and asked if he could help out. Dane's answer was a resounding "yes," before he realized he'd never even touched a professional broadcast camera before! He'd only been in a television studio as a guest showing off his ugly dog. The camera loved him, and before long Dane enrolled in De Anza College's prestigious Television & Film Program in Northern California, where he earned a degree in TV/Film Tele-Communications. He began acting and producing his own comedy and interview shows, established his own company, Tri-D Film & Video Productions, and became associated with Total Entertainment News (TEN).

Dane went on to do interviews and photo assignments for *Access Hollywood*, E!, *Hard Copy* and *20/20*, and has interviewed such notables as Kevin Costner, Clint Eastwood, former vice-president Dan Quayle and a host of others. And he is well known for his dog-like pursuit and interview with the infamous O.J. Simpson just prior to the murders, which was aired on *Inside Edition* and *American Journal*. Dane's celebrity photos have appeared in *USA Today*, *Palm Springs Life*, *People*, *Newsweek* and *Rolling Stone* magazines. Closer to home, he handles interviews and photos every year at the Palm Springs Film Festival for Total Entertainment News.

Dane's dog, Rascal, his seven-pound, naturally hairless, toothless, freckled, tongue-hanging, asymmetrical-faced Chinese Crested has won more Ugly Dog contests than any other dog in history. He's been called a space alien, Hairless Potter and Bat-dog. "But, doggone it," says Dane proudly, "ugly is in the eye of the beholder. He's drop-dead gorgeous to me and I love him!" Rascal comes from a family dynasty of ugly dogs. Mom and Grandma are title holders and Grandpa Chi-Chi is listed in the *Guinness Book of World Records*. Dane, who has been doggedly showing and competing for thirty-three years, plans to submit Rascal for the record book since he has now surpassed Grandpa in titles.

Barbara Walters has interviewed Dane and Rascal, and they have guested with Jay Leno, Donald Trump and Carson Daly, and appeared on cable television's Animal Planet five times. Rascal's recent triumphs include a first-place win at the 15th Annual Ugly Dog Contest at Del Mar Fairgrounds in Southern California, the Highland Ugly Dog Contest and a Ring of Champions title at the Fort Bragg, North Carolina, Ugly Dog Contest and, I'm told, a few horror movie producers are knocking on his doghouse door.

Andrew is producing a documentary feature film entitled *The Ugliest Dog*, which includes cameo appearances by Robin Williams, Dr. Phil, Ray Romano and Loni Anderson. He is co-starring in a 35mm film entitled *The Profile*.

He devotes much of his time and talent to raising money for Guide Dogs of the Desert and The Humane Society and his exclusive, patented Hot Dog Leash will be marketed, with a portion of sales going to animal rescue. "I'm looking forward to more acting and being able to bring awareness to animal rights so I can make a difference in society," he says. "I hope to become the person my dog thinks I am!"

To see Dane Andrew's star dedication ceremony, go to Google Video/Dane Andrew and for more info on Rascal, see *theworldsugliestdog.com*.

Bill Asher, collecting signatures at his star party.

*LOVED BY LUCY
AND BEWITCHED BY ELIZABETH*

WILLIAM ASHER

STAR #241
DEDICATED NOVEMBER 22, 2003
100 NO. PALM CANYON DR.

Bill Asher was born to be in show business...his father was Hollywood producer Ephraim Asher, who made the classic Dracula and Frankenstein movies, and his mother was actress Lillian Bonner. Starting in the studio mailroom at Universal, Bill quickly moved up to assistant editor and then assistant cameraman. He interested a producer of movie shorts in some stories he wrote and wound up directing them and was on track to his long and successful career.

Desi Arnaz noticed his talent and was so impressed he asked Bill to direct *Our Miss Brooks*, but after only a few episodes Arnaz put him on the mega-hit *I Love Lucy*. Bill's flair for staging physical comedy would be the hallmark of the 110 episodes he directed from 1951-1957. Bill moved on to direct dozens of Desilu shows, including *Make Room for Daddy* (which became *The Danny Thomas Show*) and *December Bride*. Then came *The Dinah Shore Chevy Show* for which he won an Emmy, followed by the long-running, very popular series *Bewitched*, which garnered him another Emmy. By this time, Bill was married to Elizabeth Montgomery and, through their company, Ashmont Productions, she starred in and he produced, directed or wrote all 218 episodes of *Bewitched*, which ran for eight seasons. Among his hundreds of other producing and directing credits are *Harper Valley, PTA* with Barbara Eden, *Private Benjamin* with Lorna Patterson, *Gidget* with Sally Field, *The Patty Duke Show*, the feature film *Johnny Cool* (where he met Elizabeth), and several of the popular Beach Party movies with Frankie Avalon and Annette Funicello. Bill also produced and directed *The Paul Lynde Show* and *Temperatures Rising*, which I worked on as his production secretary and for which my late writer/husband wrote scripts.

When Bill directed the television series *The Thin Man*, he became friends with its star, Peter Lawford, which led to a close association with the Kennedys. Yes, those Kennedys. He directed John F. Kennedy's 1961 Inaugural Gala, which was produced by Frank Sinatra. Joseph Kennedy then asked Bill to direct the famous JFK 45th surprise birthday party gala at Madison Square Garden in which Marilyn Monroe, in her sultry voice, sang "Happy Birthday, Mr. President." It was one of her last public appearances. As a matter of little-known fact, Bill was with Marilyn Monroe on the day she died. They spent that day as guests of Peter Lawford at his Malibu beach house. Later that evening, after Peter repeatedly called Bill to say he couldn't reach Marilyn by phone at her home, it was finally learned that she was dead.

In Bill's extensive home library sits hundreds of leather-bound books containing a thousand or so scripts he has directed, written or produced, about two-dozen nominations for *Bewitched*, *I Love Lucy* and awards from the National Academy of Television Arts & Sciences, a Golden Circle Award for his 50-plus years in television, the American Advertising Federation Award for Creative Genius in Television and the Walk of Stars Lifetime Achievement Award.

Bill met his wife, Meredith, in the desert in 1996, and it was a good thing for her in more ways than one. She had dreamed of being an actress or a singer and, with Bill, she's met almost everyone in show business she's ever hoped to meet. No word, though, on her singing or acting career.

Bill Asher's much-deserved star sits appropriately right next to the life-size bronze statue of Lucille Ball in downtown Palm Springs. His autobiography is nearing completion.

Ted Bacino celebrates.

TO BE OR NOT TO BE...
DID HE OR DIDN'T HE?

TED BACINO

STAR #259
DEDICATED NOVEMBER 2, 2005
156 N. PALM CANYON DR.

Director extraordinaire Ted Bacino enjoys a career which dates back to his college days at Northern Illinois University, where he wrote and directed the school's first-ever musical, *Take It from the Top*.

In the Army in Germany, he directed training films and servicemen's interviews. Following his Army stint, he returned to his hometown of Rockford, Illinois, to direct for the renowned Starlight Theater at Rock Valley Community College. Ted later became their PR director and also booked the Coronado Performing Arts Center and helped sell out all 2,400 seats.

Ted directed such celebrated productions as *Man of La Mancha*, *Fiddler On The Roof*, *The King and I*, and *My Fair Lady* to name a few. He coached and started the careers of a number of drama and music students who have moved on to award-winning careers. Among his protégés are producer Robert Greenblatt (*Six Feet Under*), Broadway director and actor Joe Mantello (*Wicked*), New York stage actress and singer Marin Mazzie (*Kiss Me Kate*) and music director Kevin Stites (*The Color Purple*).

In the early '90s Bacino came to the desert "for the weather," he says. "I came to retire, but my retirement was a failure." He brought the first musical, *Cabaret*, to the now-shuttered Top Hat Playhouse, which starred local favorite Justin Blake as the male lead. "We sold out every night," Blake proudly recalls. Ted wrote and directed *Red Hot & New* at the Rock

Garden Café, which ran for six months and starred another area favorite, Ed Harbour.

After fifty years of directing, I asked Ted for his best advice: "Most directors don't understand the importance of pace and inflection, but primarily pace. It's an absolute law: first act, one hour and fifteen, second act, forty-five. The show can never be too short. It has to move."

Ted speaking about his book.

A go-where-you-wanna-go, do-what-you-wanna-do kind of guy, Ted, who loves Europe, owns homes in Venice, Paris and Palm Springs. The rotation is three months in Palm Springs, two in Italy and one in France.

A few years ago, while browsing a bookstore in Venice, Ted found nothing to read, so he went home and began writing something to read. The result is his recently-published book, *The Shakespeare Conspiracy*, which deals with the age-old debate regarding William Shakespeare not being the actual writer of the world-famous Shakespearean plays. "It's the story of the greatest literary deception of all time based entirely on historical facts," he says. "In his will, Shakespeare left plates, spoons, clothes and other household items. No books. If he owned them, he would have left them. Some plays were written in Italian which Shakespeare couldn't read."

"I had been fascinated with this subject for years," he continued. "I wrote it as a play, but it was too widespread for a stage production, so I wrote it as a feature script. Then industry people told me if I write it as a book, they'll turn it into a movie, and it's selling well." Producer and Walk of Stars president Bob Alexander has optioned the property and is in negotiations with a production company to make the movie. So, did he or didn't he? Read the book and you decide. To learn more, go to *shakespeareconspiracy.com*.

Ted Bacino has been inducted into the prestigious Italian-American Hall of Fame, honoring those individuals who have made significant contributions to the arts and to other appropriate categories.

Gorgeous Carroll Baker posing for a studio PR shot.

FROM BABY DOLL TO GRANDMA
CARROLL BAKER

STAR #206
DEDICATED MAY 4, 2001
100 MUSEUM DR.

You may be surprised to learn that Carroll Baker started out as a Sorceress! Well…maybe more like a Lady Magician. She performed in Florida on the vaudeville circuit as The Magic Jewel Act, and later entered and won the Miss Florida Fruits & Vegetables contest. Then came work as a dancer in New York City, television commercials and a walk-on in a Broadway play.

Uncovering no luck with her magic act in New York, Carroll gave away all her tricks and enrolled in the prestigious Actors Studio, *the* place to be at the time. Word went out to casting directors that there was a beautiful and talented girl in town and she was offered a role on Broadway in *All Summer Long*. Producers noticed, and began casting her in films. Her first important role was opposite her pal from the Actors Studio, James Dean, in the classic film *Giant*. But Carroll's big break turned up when she auditioned for the renowned filmmaker Elia Kazan and Tennessee Williams for the lead role in the notorious film *Baby Doll*. She was cast as the teenage, thumb-sucking bride of Karl Malden, which earned her a well-deserved Oscar nomination. The picture was condemned by the Legion of Decency and launched her as a major movie star and a Hollywood sex symbol.

Carroll went on to star in numerous motion pictures such as *The Big Country*, *How The West Was Won*, *The Carpetbaggers*, *The Greatest Story Ever Told* and *Harlow*, to name a few. While shooting the film *Mister Moses* on location in Africa, she caught the eye of a Masai Chieftan, who offered the studio 150 cows, 200 goats and sheep and $750 in trade for her, but no deal was ever made, possibly because her agent couldn't use ten percent of cows, goats and sheep!

When her fourteen-year marriage to director Jack Garfein ended and when, at the same time, she became involved in a legal battle with Paramount Pictures, Carroll moved to Italy with her two children. She remained there for ten years and continued her career, starring in scores of European films that took her to locations all over the world, making her a global celebrity.

She's worked with such leading men as Jack Nicholson, Robert Mitchum, Jimmy Stewart, Arnold Schwarzenegger and Clark Gable, of whom she says, "When he kissed me, they had to carry me off the set!" She's been nominated six times for her performances, won a Golden Globe, a Laurel Award, a Golden Boot Award, and has been featured in *Playboy, Look* and *Life* magazines, but says, "What I'm most proud of are my two grown children and six grandchildren." Her daughter, Blanche Baker, is an Emmy Award-winning actress and son Herschel Garfein is a theatrical composer, writer and stage director for musical theatre.

Carroll Baker has been awarded two stars…one on the Hollywood Walk of Fame and one on the Palm Springs Walk of Stars. Her autobiography, fittingly titled *Baby Doll*, is available at amazon.com.

Kaye Ballard.

SHE LOST 10 POUNDS IN 53 YEARS!

KAYE BALLARD

STAR #52
DEDICATED NOVEMBER 18, 1995
101 SO. PALM CANYON DRIVE

She lives on Kaye Ballard Lane in the house formerly owned by Desi Arnaz. If you need directions, she'll tell you, "Go down Bob Hope Drive, past Dinah Shore, past Gerald Ford, but don't cross Frank Sinatra!"

Comedienne, singer, actress, and author Catherine Gloria Balotta, aka Kaye Ballard, was born in Cleveland, Ohio, to Italian immigrants and was bitten by the performing bug by age five. Growing up in a house full of laughter, she always thought funny and was the class and family clown. She would dance and sing her way around the kitchen floor for anyone who'd watch and listen. While still a teenager, Kaye performed in a USO production of *Stage Door Canteen*, then came vaudeville and burlesque houses. Funny guy Spike Jones found her ushering in a theatre and put her on his tour singing, playing tuba and doing her wonderful comedy impressions. Kaye briefly performed with the Vaughan Monroe and Stan Kenton bands and made her way to Broadway, appearing in *Three to Make Ready* in 1946, followed by the musical *Once in a Lifetime* and later *The Golden Apple*, *Pirates of Penzance* and many more. Years later, Kaye's stage work included *Nunsense*, *Funny Girl*, and *The Full Monty*. More recently, Kaye entertained delighted audiences as the star of the *Palm Springs Follies* at the famed Plaza Theatre in downtown Palm Springs.

She also created a comedy-and-song nightclub act which she brought to the Blue Angel in New York, the Persian Room at the Plaza Hotel, Mr.

Kelly's in Chicago and the Hungry I in San Francisco (the "I" stands for intelligent). At Hollywood's Mocambo on the Sunset Strip, Kaye would do her impressions of James Cagney, Bette Davis, Joan Crawford and others. At times Ethel Merman or Judy Garland would be in the audience shouting out, "Do me! Do me!"

In 1954, Kaye graced the cover of *Life* magazine. Every talk and variety television show host wanted her as a guest, including Ed Sullivan, Steve Allen, Carol Burnett, Merv Griffin and Bob Hope. She made hundreds of appearances on Johnny Carson's *Tonight Show*. In television, Kaye guest-starred in such hit shows as *Laugh-In, Fantasy Island, The Love Boat, Here's Lucy* and was a regular on *The Doris Day Show* for one season, but may be best remembered for her role as Kaye Buell in the popular '60s sitcom *The Mothers-in-Law* with Eve Arden, which was produced by Desi Arnaz. "I got that role," she says, "because Lucille Ball saw me in a New York club and said, 'You're funny'!" Phyllis Diller agreed, saying, "She's on my short list of funny people." Ballard's film credits include *A House Is Not a Home* with Shelley Winters, *Freaky Friday* with Jodi Foster and *The Ritz*, with Rita Moreno and Jerry Stiller.

Kaye and me during her talk at the Palm Springs Women's Press Club.

She has completed the audio version of her warmhearted and humorous memoir, *How I Lost 10 Pounds in 53 Years*. The book and audio version is available at Amazon.com. A breast cancer survivor, she says, "Life is wonderful now…I do what I want, which includes seeing lots of movies and enjoying my four dogs…two Shih Tzus, a poodle and a Lhasa Apso." The First Lady of Entertainment, Kaye Ballard is not only still here… she's still available!

A glamorous Miss Rona.

RONA BARRETT'S HOLLYWOOD

RONA BARRETT

STAR #323
DEDICATED OCTOBER 9, 2009
111 S. PALM CANYON DR.

The sun'll come out tomorrow! And so will the stars…and they came out to see Rona Barrett become the 323rd recipient on the Walk of Stars.

When, as a young child, Rona overheard her doctor advising her parents that she could die at an early age because of a diagnosis of Muscular Dystrophy, she didn't believe it. "No. I'm not going to die," she said. "Famous people don't die!"

Driven by an intense desire to make something of herself, Rona studied journalism at New York University, having switched from pre-Law. She went to work for a movie magazine and quickly advanced from secretary to assistant editor. Fascinated with all things show business, Rona wanted to write only about celebrities. She met famed Hollywood producer Robert Evans, who introduced her to the editor of *Photoplay* magazine and she was off to Hollywood. After a few years, Rona realized that none of the news programs were reporting on the entertainment industry and, not satisfied with being just another columnist, she set out knocking on every network door, but with no success. She called Dad in New York to say she was coming back home. He convinced her not to quit, to give it twenty-four hours more, and in that time she wrote a letter to the president of ABC saying in part, "Yea or nay…will you put me on TV?" The manager of KABC-TV in L.A. called to say they'd try her out. Dad proudly said, "See, I told you so!" And Rona Barrett became the first person to bring entertainment reporting to television.

So there she was, an on-air entertainment reporter in the mid-sixties, with her own segment called *Hollywood Report by Rona Barrett*, at a time when only a handful of women were in broadcasting. She later became the first entertainment journalist on *Good Morning, America, The Today Show* and *Entertainment Tonight*, and edited several fan magazines, including *Rona Barrett's Hollywood*. She published her own newsletter, three books and her up-close-and-personal autobiography, *Miss Rona*. The pioneer of celebrity journalism, Rona got to the heart and soul of these A-List celebrities with her incisive and intimate questioning. "It was simply intense curiosity," she says. "I was driven to understand what makes them tick, to see what was reel and what was real."

A recently-released DVD is available entitled *Rona Barrett's Hollywood — Nothing but the Truth*, which includes Rona's most sensational, in-depth celebrity interviews of the '70s with John Wayne, Richard Dreyfus, Cher, Robin Williams, John Travolta, Carol Burnett and others. One dollar from each DVD sale will be donated to The Rona Barrett Foundation, an organization she founded, which is dedicated to helping the elderly in need and born out of her experience in caring for her ailing father who passed away at age 96. Learn more at *ronabarrettfoundation.org*. The DVD is available at Amazon, Borders and Barnes & Noble.com.

No stranger to Palm Springs, Rona started vacationing there in the late '50s, fell in love with the desert and bought a home in Elvis Presley's neighborhood and was the first reporter to uncover the story of his marriage to Priscilla.

The legendary Rona Barrett has left her mark in break-out journalism and now leaves her mark on the Walk of Stars!

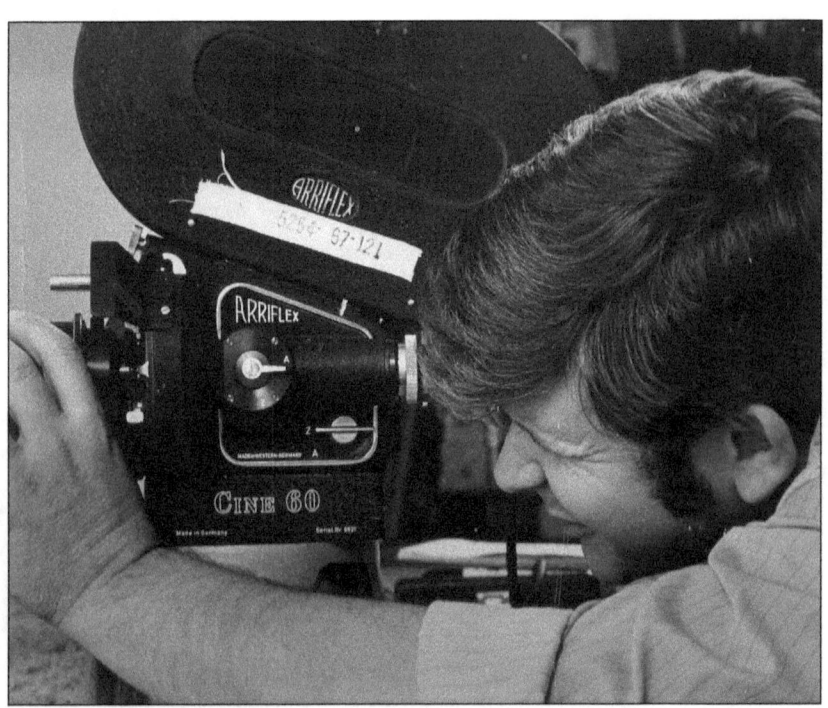
Cliff Bole checks a shot.

*FROM MISSION IMPOSSIBLE
TO MISSION ACCOMPLISHED*

CLIFF BOLE

STAR #253
DEDICATED APRIL 23, 2005
254 SO. PALM CANYON DR.

As kids growing up, most of us were probably sometimes told to go out and play in the backyard. Not so with director Cliff Bole...his backyard was backstage, and one of his play toys was Charlie McCarthy, ventriloquist Edgar Bergen's dummy. Not to mention a few grown-up pals like Eddie Cantor, Jimmy Durante and Bob Hope. The only picture Cliff has of his dad, in his mind or in a frame, is in a tuxedo. Dad ran the famed Golden Gate Theatre in San Francisco.

The family moved to Southern California when Dad became studio manager at Universal Pictures. When the family wasn't spending weekends in Palm Springs, Cliff and his buddies would sneak into the Universal, Warner Bros. and Republic backlots and endlessly watch filming on the soundstages. "I never was interested in the actors," he says. "I was fascinated with the director on the set."

After high school, Bole started out in the studio mailroom and later found work as a stuntman before moving to script supervisor, then first assistant director. His first actual directing jobs were on commercials, and his big break came on *The Six Million Dollar Man* when the director suddenly quit. Lee Majors suggested Bole and he was on track for his long and successful career.

He's one of the lucky people who got to work in a business they love, and with the biggest names; Kirk Douglas, Marilyn Monroe, Clark Gable, Richard Burton and Marlon Brando to name a few. On location most of his early years, he worked a sixteen-hour day. Among Bole's credits are *The X-Files, Mission: Impossible, Fantasy Island, Charlie's Angels, The Six Million Dollar Man, Hart to Hart* and *Emergency!* But he's best known for his sixteen-year stint on one of the most popular names in science-fiction entertainment, *Star Trek*, including all five spinoffs. The *Star Trek* aliens, the Bolian race, were named after Bole, as was the scenic tourist spot on their home planet, The Cliffs of Bole.

I asked him to describe what he does: "Directing is the greatest joy I can think of," replies Bole. "The script is the blueprint and I'm the architect. I deal with a different subject every seven days and have control over the end product. In 7-10 days of prep, I take the script and divide each scene into cinematic shots and shoot it accordingly. If it's an unproduceable script, I go to the producers and have it rewritten or throw it out. If it's too expensive to produce, we make cuts in the production meeting. First to go are the extras…if there are a hundred, we cut them to ten, and shoot the scene to make it look like a hundred. Today's shows have more production values. What cost $300,000 an episode years ago, now costs $2-5 million."

I asked if he ever invites the scriptwriter to the set: "Sure, but I stopped. You can only be tapped on the shoulder so many times." He once had a dispute over how to play a scene with William Shatner on the cop show *T.J. Hooker*. "You're no longer my favorite director," Shatner said. "You've never been my favorite actor," Bole countered. One of them was temporarily fired.

Cliff Bole's best advice on directing: "Start at the top. There's no such thing as advancing from the mailroom anymore. Either come out of college with a film degree, or come from a writing background. And oh, yes…nepotism still works."

Recently, Cliff directed *Murder Mystery Dinner Theater* and is considering an offer to teach at University of Riverside. When not working, he takes time for golf and flying a plane or just enjoying life with wife Brenda. From weekends to full time in Palm Springs and what once seemed like a mission impossible, became a mission accomplished.

Golden Girl, Pattie Daly Caruso.

GOLD IN HER HEART AND IN HER HANDS
PATTIE DALY CARUSO

STAR #252
DEDICATED MARCH 19, 2005
265 S. PALM CANYON DR.

She's the gold standard in spokespersons! "As an integral part of the Coachella Valley, Pattie Daly Caruso has the talent and the energy to represent our company," says Rob Riddle Moser, owner of Out of the Box Gold Store in Palm Desert, California. "She's very genuine." With gold in her hands as well as in her heart, Pattie can be seen daily in print ads in the local newspaper, on ten billboards around town and on CBS-TV and Time-Warner Cable.

Pattie wanted to become an actress, but there were no movie studios in Fayetteville, North Carolina, so at the young age of seventeen she discovered radio, writing commercials and hosting her own show called *Pat's Platter Party*, at a time when there were no women on the station.

She went to the Los Angeles area to attend the famed Pasadena Playhouse and after graduation found acting and dancing roles and toured the United States and Canada with the musical variety show *Shindig*. Pattie married Jim Daly and produced daughter Quinn and son Carson. She continued her career writing and producing commercials as marketing director for station KSRF in Santa Monica, California, although placing it second to her kids' needs. Widowed at a young age, Pattie married Richard Caruso, and welcomed his sons Tony and Rick into her life and moved to the desert. There, she unselfishly got busy working with the charities Shelter from the Storm, the Ronald McDonald House and, as a breast cancer survivor, Gilda's Club, The American Cancer Society and more.

Through her production company, PDC Entertainment, Pattie hosts the longest-running local television talk show, *Valley Views*, which formerly ran seven days a week and now airs as periodic specials four times a year on KPSP-2. Pattie covers local events, lifestyles and celebrity interviews.

Pattie has hosted hundreds of events, including Desert Samaritans' Annual "Faith 'n Begora" St. Patrick's Day lunch, and the Annual Theresa A. Mike Scholarship Fund Fashion Show sale and dinner.

Among Pattie's numerous awards are Television Woman of the Year, First Lady of the Desert, the prestigious Athena Award, Desert Woman of the Year, one of David Letterman's Top Ten Moms, and she was featured on MTV's *Celebrity Moms*. Recently, the Desert Samaritans recognized her tireless efforts for others when she received the Good Samaritan of the Year Award.

Several years ago, Pattie founded the group Media Mavens, along with media gals Judy Vossler and Janet Newcomb. Realizing that the women in print, radio and television she hung out with were not very well connected, she cleverly thought up the opportunity for them to get together and network, like meeting once a month at various restaurants in town.

Career-wise, Pattie "has things to share" and will be writing a book, but for now she just wants to enjoy her grandchildren. "It's so great," she says, "these grandchildren are like seeing your kids all over again…like little replicas of my kids, Quinn and Carson. Dad always said the most important thing is to learn how to think and reason for yourself and I've passed that on to my own children." Pattie's motto is "Live in the now moment," and has recently added a familiar favorite: "It is what it is!"

Carol Channing.

WELL, HELLO, CAROL!
STILL GLOWIN', STILL CROWIN',
STILL GOIN' STRONG!

CAROL CHANNING

STAR #331
DEDICATED OCTOBER 2, 2010
369 N. PALM CANYON DR.

Our legendary First Lady of Musical Theater first stepped on a stage while helping her mother deliver newspapers to theaters backstage in her hometown of San Francisco. As she stood on the darkened stage, she thought, "This is where I want to be!" She explained, "I was an only child and because of loneliness, I brought home, in my imagination, every classmate who was interesting to me."

Following high school, Carol attended Bennington College, a private liberal arts school in Vermont where she studied drama and dance, and then set out for New York to pursue her dream. Her first stage job was *No for an Answer*, followed by several other major productions. After many featured roles, she toured the nightclub circuit and later appeared in numerous films and television shows.

In her first breakout role, *Gentlemen Prefer Blondes*, Carol introduced her signature song: "Diamonds Are a Girl's Best Friend." She says, "That's when I realized I made it. They made me a star." Carol is best remembered for her role as Dolly Gallagher in Jerry Herman's *Hello, Dolly!* Having starred in the role over 5,000 times, she never missed a performance! "Well, maybe one-half a performance," she allows. "In Kalamazoo I got food poisoning, and did a few shows in a wheelchair. One night I fell in the orchestra pit. I called out to the musicians to keep playing, ran around and out the stage door where the guard asked who I was. 'Carol Channing,'

I said breathlessly, and he said, 'Yeah, sure.' I ran around to the front door, ran down the aisle to the stage and the dancers pulled me up!"

I asked where this incredible work ethic comes from: "You can't disappoint the audience. You reach to the heavens to get the show out!" Ever the trouper, not even ovarian cancer treatment in the '70s kept her away from a performance.

Carol Channing on stage.

Carol has collected perhaps a hundred awards, including three Tony's, one of which is for Lifetime Achievement, the Actors' Fund Award, an Academy Award nomination, a Golden Globe Award and an Honorary Doctorate in Fine Arts from California State University Stanislaus. "A doctor who makes house calls," she quips. "These days, they don't know what to do with me, so they give me an award." Her diamond dress worn in *Gentlemen Prefer Blondes* and her red-sequined dress worn in *Hello, Dolly!*, are on display at the Smithsonian Institute.

Carol and husband Harry Killijian's storybook romance began when they were junior high school sweethearts about seventy-six years ago. They went on to different high schools and other marriages, but never forgot each other. In 2003 a mutual friend reunited them and within four weeks they were married. The happy couple spends half the year in Modesto, California, where Harry, a land developer, bought a farm fifty-

Carol and me when she spoke and performed for the Palm Springs Women's Press Club.

five years ago. The other half is spent in Rancho Mirage, California, where Channing has entertained, sometimes accompanied by my late musician husband, Whitey Mitchell.

They have embarked on a national campaign to restore the arts back into public schools through their non-profit organization, The Dr. Carol Channing and Harry Killijian Foundation for the Arts, which is dedicated to preserving arts education in public schools and to providing scholarships to students. She says, "It's got to be included in education. It makes the students' brains more facile when they're exposed to the arts. They perform better academically and it strengthens their self-esteem." Carol was honored for her efforts in the California state legislature by Governor Arnold Schwarzenegger and a Congressional resolution expressing support has passed in the House and is now in the Senate. Carol and Harry would like to expand this program nationally. To learn more or to donate to this worthy cause, go to *carolchanning.org*.

Carol's new CD, titled *For Heaven's Sake*, includes Americana and spiritual songs she learned from her father. Her candid autobiography, *Just Lucky, I Guess-A Memoir of Sorts*, chronicles a career that has spanned over seven decades in show business. Both can be ordered at Amazon.com.

Carol on star day. I'm in the second row, sunglasses on.

First performed in 2003, Carol has toured the country with her one-woman show, *The First 80 Years Are the Hardest*, a retrospective of her life in word and song. She's joined Harry as a nonagenarian and he says the show will be retitled *The First 90 Years…*

Carol Channing's shining star will always be there to remind us…It's so nice to have her back where she belongs!

Carol Connors. What a knockout!

GOING THE DISTANCE
CAROL CONNORS

STAR #143
DEDICATED JANUARY 16, 1999
275 S. PALM CANYON DR.

She bought her house for a song…literally. As Rocky Balboa, played by Sylvester Stallone, ran up the steps of the Philadelphia Art Museum and did a victory dance, Carol Connors laughed as she walked all the way to the bank. As co-writer of "Gonna Fly Now," the theme song from the blockbuster movie *Rocky*, Carol was paid a paltry $500 up front and bought her home on the backend deal!

She grew up with the gift of song. Her mom studied at Poland's Warsaw Conservatory and taught Carol all the arias from *Carmen, Rigoletto, Madame Butterfly* and others. Carol even dared to rewrite Beethoven at an early age and at twelve she penned her first song. In high school, Carol's classmate was, you should excuse the expression, the infamous Phil Spector, with whom she formed a vocal group trio known as The Teddy Bears. They each put up $10 and raised $30 to cut the hit record "To Know Him Is to Love Him," which rose to number one on the *Billboard* charts. Carol went on to co-write an American car song classic hit, "Hey Little Cobra."

Then came a dry spell in the '60s when not much happened career-wise. Carol pounded the pavement and knocked on every door. "I lived in a cave," she recalls. "It was carved right into the mountain in L.A.'s Laurel Canyon area." She had the talent and the persistence, she just needed the luck and, boy, did she get it! "My agent sent me the *Rocky* shooting script and told me to go to the UA/MGM studio screening room to see the rough cut. They were all there…Sylvester Stallone, John Avildsen the director, Bill Conti the composer, producers Chartoff & Winkler, and the lyricist Ayn Robbins. As we watched Rocky Balboa sprint through Philadelphia with no music, just dialogue, someone stood up and shouted, 'You're all gonna get nominated for an Oscar!' Then someone else stood up and yelled, 'You're all gonna be propelled into stardom!' I began to think something big was happening here, went home, got into the shower and got it! I called Bill Conti from the shower and said, 'I got it! I know what the film's about!'" And the rest, as they say, is history.

As predicted, *Rocky* did receive numerous awards, as did Carol…several Emmy and Oscar nominations as well as Gold and Platinum Records. Her other film and television work includes music and lyrics for *Looking For Mr. Goodbar*, *Dressed To Kill*, *The Onion Field*, Walt Disney's *The Rescuers*, *Lifestyles of the Rich and Famous*, *Star Search* and more.

Although by choice never married, Carol's had some exceptionally renowned boyfriends: Elvis Presley, David Janssen and Robert Culp. She says she's the happiest sitting at the piano staring at a blank piece of paper when the idea comes to her and she can't write it down fast enough! By the way, that house she bought for a song…it's in Beverly Hills, near her neighbor and friend Sylvester Stallone.

Carol gives much of her time and talent to charities such as the Asthma-Allergy Foundation and Society of Singers and commits to at least two events; Celebrity Host of Tony Aguilar's Annual Greater Palm Springs Celebrity Golf Classic in December of each year, and Guest Entertainer at columnist Gloria Greer's ACT For MS Annual Stroll Down Christmas Tree Lane event in December.

Michael Dante.

ONE CANNOT DICTATE TO THE HEART

MICHAEL DANTE

STAR #33
DEDICATED JUNE 19, 1994
114 S. PALM CANYON DR.

Michael Dante, who used to be Ralph Vitti, started life in a sports-minded family in Stamford, Connecticut. "All energy was directed toward athletics," he says. "Even still I was fascinated with all things Western…its history and lore, and always found time to play Cowboys & Indians."

Michael played on his high-school baseball team and after graduation signed with the Boston Braves (now Atlanta Braves) as a bonus ballplayer. With his $6,000 windfall, he bought his family a new car. Later, Michael moved to Orlando to play with the Washington Senators (now Minnesota Twins) and, while there, took drama classes at the University of Miami. He met and hung out with famed bandleader Tommy Dorsey, a huge baseball fan, who took a liking to Michael and was able to arrange a screen test in Hollywood. Once there, Michael tested with MGM, signed a contract and never looked back.

Baseball's loss was Hollywood's gain. His first film was *Somebody Up There Likes Me*, with Paul Newman and then-unknown Steve McQueen. A lot of somebodys down here liked him, too. During his Hollywood years he was under contract with three studios: MGM, Warner Bros. and 20th Century-Fox. The camera loved Michael Dante. He appeared in over 30 feature films and 150 television shows, including two movies with World War II's most decorated hero, Audie Murphy, *Apache Rifles* and *Arizona*

Raiders, as well as *Kid Galahad* with Elvis Presley, *The Legend of Custer* with Slim Pickens and the classic drama *The Naked Kiss*.

Dante considers his work in *Winterhawk*, in which he played the title role, among his best. "Winterhawk was the leader of a nation," Dante recalls. "Beyond the script as written, I made him a spiritual man. The decisions I made as that character were not based on ego, they were always related to the elements." He owns the sequel and ancillary rights to *Winterhawk* and is in the throes of obtaining financing.

Michael's television work includes *The Six Million Dollar Man, Maverick, Bonanza, The Texan, Cagney & Lacey, Get Smart,* and recurring roles on *Days of Our Lives* and *General Hospital*, among others. He frequently appeared on *Star Trek* and regularly attends Trekkie conventions. *The Michael Dante Celebrity Talk Show* was heard on the radio for many years. His VIP guest list included Milton Berle, Ernie Borgnine, Tony Curtis, Phyllis Diller, Charlton Heston, and, from the sports world, Hall of Famers Yogi Berra, Tommy Lasorda and many more.

A few of Dante's many awards are the Golden Boot Award (Western actors' equivalent to an Oscar), the Silver Spur Award (the Golden Globe of the Western genre) and a Palm Springs Festival Award. His star on the Walk of Stars is thoughtfully positioned between two of his Warner Bros. cohorts, Connie Stevens and executive producer William T. Orr.

The Dantes' sprawling ranch-style home is jam-packed with an impressive collection of American Western artifacts, memorabilia, paintings and handiworks he's amassed during his lengthy career. He's the proud owner of a Remington bronze statue titled "The Rattlesnake," an authentic hunting bow & hatchet, the saddle he used as well as the framed buckskin vest worn while filming *Winterhawk*, and a hand-carved wood statue of Indian war chief Sitting Bull and one of the Native-American Crazy Horse, both presented to him by the original artists.

These days Michael attends Western film festivals, star conventions and celebrity charity golf tournaments. He's still an athlete and will most likely crush you on the golf course. For many years he hosted his own tournament.

A favorite line of dialogue Michael spoke to Audie Murphy in *Apache Rifles* is "One cannot dictate to the heart," and he's taken that advice. He and wife Mary Jane have been heartily on cloud nine for over eighteen years.

Kal David and Lauri Bono entertain their many fans.

THEY ARE THE REAL DEAL

KAL DAVID & LAURI BONO

STAR #248
DEDICATED DECEMBER 5, 2004
120 S. PALM CANYON DR.

If you're a musician and you play the Blues, you better play the tune "Sweet Home Chicago," and nobody does it better than Kal David, and not just because he was born and raised there.

Kal was given a guitar by his uncle at age eleven, and in high school and beyond he formed various bands. His first hit record was with his group The Fabulous Rhinestones.

Lauri, who was raised in Waterbury, Connecticut, found her calling early on. By age four, at her large family gatherings, she'd sing standing on the kitchen table surrounded by several singing and dancing uncles and her dad. She, too, had a high-school band, later formed a jazz group and toured up and down the New England coast. She moved to Woodstock, New York, in her twenties and sang with her band in local clubs. Kal, who was on tour in the area, heard about a great singer and went in to hear her. "I was so impressed personally as well as professionally," he recalls, "I asked her to perform on my demo record." And the real deal began… only they didn't call it that yet.

Kal and Lauri relocated to Los Angeles where they found work touring with the legendary blues singer Etta James, as well as the great Johnny Rivers. Later, Lauri did a stint as a backup singer for Bette Midler. In L.A., they were in demand all over town, including Le Café in Sherman Oaks where they recorded a Johnny Rivers-produced CD, *Live at Le Café*, and generously donated the proceeds to the charity Comic Relief. Now a fourteen-piece band known as Kal & Lauri and the Dream Band, Featuring Steve Madaio, they continued their successful run in Hollywood and landed a dream gig at the hottest, hippest nitery in town, The China Club, and Kal became musical director, hosting the Pro Jam on Monday nights. The club attracted such mega-stars as Stevie Wonder, Elton John, George Harrison, Julian Lennon and others.

In the mid-'90s, after touring Europe, Kal and Lauri opened their own club, The Blue Guitar, in the heart of downtown Palm Springs. Now, known as Kal David & The Real Deal, featuring Lauri Bono, they managed and performed in the club six nights a week. "I cooked the food, cleaned up, did the laundry and the payroll," Lauri said, "but it became too difficult to run a club from the bandstand." So, after six successful years, they closed the club. On closing night, they not only recorded their CD *Live At The Blue Guitar*, but learned that their many fans, friends and employees were about to present them with their own star, which sits directly in front of their former club. When Lauri brought her parents to see the star, a tearful Mom said, "This is the greatest thing that's ever happened to our family!"

No longer constrained by the demands as performing club owners, Kal and Lauri took to the road again, appearing at all the major jazz and blues festivals in Toronto, Calgary, Alaska, the Caribbean, Connecticut, Boston and Atlanta.

Kal has been performing for over fifty years now, twenty-three of them with Lauri and their love and commitment to their music and to each other is evident. They *are* the real deal.

Tom Dreesen.

*HE TELLS JOKES, HE PLAYS GOLF...
LIFE IS GOOD!*

TOM DREESEN

STAR #146
DEDICATED FEBRUARY 18, 1999
275 S. PALM CANYON DR.

Harvey, Illinois, on the south side of Chicago, was never a birthplace of stars, but Tom Dreesen changed all that. He's come a long way since his childhood days growing up in a rat-infested shack, one of eight children sleeping five to a bed. He waited until he was seven to go to work, shining shoes while listening to Frank Sinatra on the jukebox in his role model Uncle Frank Polizzi's bar. "Uncle Frank was a gifted storyteller," Tom says. "I was fascinated that he could unite everyone in the room with his stories and jokes, which I'd re-tell to my friends." It was good training for Dreesen who would one day become one of America's most lovable and enduring comedians.

Dreesen began his career after a stint in the Navy when he met actor Tim Reid in 1969. They began ad-libbing routines and, before long, took their act on the road. Show business' first odd couple worked together five years before retiring their partnership, but not their friendship. They've written a book titled *Tim & Tom: An American Comedy in Black & White*, which tells a compelling story about their career during a time of great racial divide in the country. An independent film company has signed with them to produce a movie based on their experiences.

Tom moved his family to L.A. to pursue his solo career and hung out at The Comedy Store where he bonded with Letterman, Leno and Robin Williams. His big break came when a *Tonight Show* producer booked him.

"You hadn't made it until you'd been on *The Tonight Show* with Johnny Carson," he says. "One appearance and I was signed to a CBS development deal…the unemployment line one day and a contract player at CBS the next!" Dreesen would return to *The Tonight Show* sixty-one times.

Soon, he was in demand all over the country. "The first time I was ever in Vegas was opening for Sammy Davis. At our first rehearsal, Sammy, seeing how nervous I was, said, 'You've earned this. You belong here. This is our house.' Then I knew I belonged. I would sit in the wings, night after night, watching and learning from him." Dreesen also toured with Tony Orlando, Mac Davis, Frankie Avalon and, more recently, Michael Buble.

Then came another big break…opening act for Frank Sinatra, a gig he would own for the next thirteen years. His fondest memories are times spent with Sinatra at his Rancho Mirage home. Dreesen recalls: "He'd stay awake until the sun came up, sipping his Jack Daniels. He'd come to my bungalow, wake me and say, 'Let's go for a ride,' and he'd reminisce. One night he got very personal. 'It's okay, Frank,' I said.' It won't go any further than this car. We're not exactly strangers,' and we burst into song, 'Strangers in the Night,' and he quickly pointed out I was off-key."

A low handicap golfer (he has a storage space full of crystal, trophies and golf bags and can boast six holes-in-one), he plays and performs/emcees in the Bob Hope Classic every year, the Frank Sinatra Invitational, the Clint Eastwood tournament, as well as Tiger Woods' tournament and, this year, the Kraft Nabisco Dinah Shore.

Dreesen headlines in Vegas, Tahoe and Atlantic City and other venues. He's made over five hundred appearances on television and is in constant demand from the corporate world as a motivational speaker and emcee. He writes his own material, teaches a comedy class at The Improv and The Laugh Factory and generously gives of his time and talent to charities, including MS in remembrance of his late sister. He's the recipient of the Ellis Island Medal of Honor for his humanitarian efforts. And, of course, his hometown of Harvey never forgot the best thing that ever happened to them…they named the street corner where he sold newspapers "Dreesen Street."

These days, Tom Dreesen continues performing his stand-up and storytelling, touring with his intimate one-man show, *An Evening of Laughter and Memories of Sinatra*, and has been moving audiences from laughter to tears and back.

"I tell jokes and I play golf," Tom quips. "Life is good. Keep laughing, especially at me!"

Joey English.

THE MOST FUN YOU CAN HAVE LISTENING TO THE RADIO
JOEY ENGLISH

STAR #193
DEDICATED: NOVEMBER 17, 2000
301 N. PALM CANYON DR.

Missouri-born Joey English began her musical journey singing in church as early as age three. Raised in the San Joaquin Valley in Central California, she attended a liberal arts college studying voice and piano. Although a classically-trained pianist, Joey's first instrument is her voice and is known in some show-business circles as a singer's singer. But that's not all…this multi-talented lady plays violin and most of the brass instruments, including French horn.

Performing on the road for some thirty years, Joey's career path includes working with such icons as George Burns, Bob Hope, Milton Berle and Rodney Dangerfield. "I learned everything I know from George Burns," she says; "how to think on my feet, how to deliver a line and comedic timing. Lighting and stage direction I learned from the best, Uncle Miltie." Joey has appeared on major network talk and variety shows hosted by Dinah Shore, Merv Griffin and Mike Douglas. She has sung the national anthem for many sporting events and recalls one fun evening: "While singing for the L.A. Kings at the Stanley Cup Playoffs, someone from the opposing team cut off the microphone cord. So two of the Kings skated over, lifted me up and skated me across the ice to another microphone. And the Kings won that game!"

If you live in or visit the desert for any length of time, you're aware of Joey English as a charismatic radio personality. For the last fifteen years

Joey has been heard broadcasting on Saturdays from 9-11AM and 4-6PM on 970, 1140 and 1250AM and 94.3FM, and streaming on the internet at *www.knewsradio.com*. She says the secret to being a good interviewer is being a good listener. "Everybody has a story. It's about them." Joey and her guests laugh their way through four jam-packed hours, while keeping listeners informed on current events, entertainment, community service, dining, and so much more. She's nicknamed "The Voice of the Desert" and it's the most fun you can have listening to the radio.

Joey co-starred in the local stage productions of *Senior Class, Sordid Lives* and *Best Little Whorehouse in Texas*. Actor/producer/athlete Fred Williamson has a television project in motion in which the two of them would star, called *He Said, She Said*. Career-wise, the only thing missing, Joey says: "I'd like to sing on Broadway."

For years Joey emceed the Walk of Stars dedications with the co-founder, the late Gerhard Frenzel, and she continues to brighten the social and charity scene. "They have only to ask, and I'll be there, especially if the charity involves children." Joey also finds time for active membership in two networking groups which meet once a month, Women in Film & Television and Media Mavens.

Mother of three children, Trevor, Tami and Tyler, and grandmother to Dalton, Shelbey, Alea and Trent, Joey proudly says, "My most challenging role was raising my kids to be accomplished, Christian, intelligent human beings…which they are!" And they were smart enough to honor Mom by sponsoring her star on the Walk of Stars!

The Evaro Family. Front; Shirley, Mom Angie, Sherry. Back; Jerry, Jimmy, Dad Sonny, Jeffrey.

THE FIRST FAMILY OF ENTERTAINMENT
SONNY EVARO & FAMILY

STAR #260
DEDICATED NOVEMBER 28, 2005
285 N. PALM CANYON DR.

Music is in their blood or, more exactly, their DNA. The Evaro family dynasty dates back to the mid-1800s where Sonny Evaro's Portuguese great-great-grandfather was a trapeze artist and violinist. Around 160 years later, Sonny arrived in Palm Springs, California, by way of Yuma, Arizona, with his wife and kids. Playing piano since age nine, Sonny entertained with his dad and brother at the legendary local celebrity hangout Howard Manor as The Evaro Trio. Then came stints at Gene Autry's, The Ritz Carlton, Ocotillo Lodge and the El Mirador (before it became a hospital). Later, Sonny found work in the L.A.-Hollywood area and Hawaii and was offered numerous gigs on the road, but, given his strong family ties, he always refused

It was at the El Mirador Hotel when the Evaros' five talented musical siblings first appeared on stage, singing and playing their own instruments. Growing up, home was filled with music, singing and laughter and in the mid-'70s, after a first-place win on *The Gong Show* with four of their cousins, an impressed agent brought the group to L.A. to sign with Roulette Records and record with Motown. Mom Angie says, "I shuttled the kids back and forth for meetings and recording sessions, just like the Partridge Family!"

The dynamic Evaros have been in constant demand for shows, concerts, and fairs…wherever good music-oriented fans gather. I individually asked them what it was like to grow up in the Evaro family and they all provided the same answer: "Loving, supportive, fun and exciting!"

Jerry, the leader who plays guitar, keyboard and drums, said, "The first band we formed was called Jerry and The Juveniles." He writes and arranges and an original album is in the works.

Jimmy, who plays conga and drums, remembers: "All of us lined up at the door as Dad left for work. He'd kiss each one of us goodnight. I thought every kid's Dad could play. I once asked a classmate where his dad was playing that night and he replied, 'He's not. He's a plumber!'"

Jerry and Jimmy perform at the local hot spot and newly-remodeled Sammy G's Tuscan Grill.

Shirley thinks back: "Mornings, I'd wake up to dad, grandfather, aunts and uncles practicing music. Dad encouraged us to be the best we can be." She recently recorded a CD, *Just Because of Jesus*. Shirley and husband Sergio often appear at the popular Hog's Breath Inn in La Quinta.

Sherry recalls: "I first performed at age five in a school talent show. I can't ever remember not singing."

Sonny remembers a time when he met Mary Pickford and Louis Armstrong. "My proudest professional moment," he tells, "is when I played 'Stardust' for Hoagy Carmichael, his most famous song…and he even thanked me!" When asked if there's anything he didn't get to do, Sonny said, "I wanted to learn how to fly." Angie quickly added, "I clipped his wings!"

The family performs all together often, including sometimes for Women In Film's Annual Broken Glass Awards.

Sonny and Angie raised five kids, boast fifteen grandchildren and eleven great-grandchildren, and recently celebrated fifty-three years of marriage! As the First Family of Entertainment, the Evaros have the distinction of being the largest group to grace one star, and if the PSWOS had one for family values, they'd own that one, too! For more, go to *www.myspace/evarofamily*.

Enticingly, Rhonda.

HER MIDDLE NAME SHOULD BE CHARITY
RHONDA FLEMING

STAR #297
DEDICATED DECEMBER 9, 2007
200 S. PALM CANYON DR.

One of the categories for induction in the Palm Springs Walk of Stars is humanitarian or philanthropist, and Marilyn Louis, who became Rhonda Fleming, qualifies in this area just as much as for her movie star status.

While her original ambition was to become a singer, Rhonda was discovered walking home from Beverly Hills High School by famed agent Henry Willson, who had seen her photo in a magazine and asked if she had ever thought of being in pictures. He arranged for her to meet the iconic Hollywood producer David O. Selznick, as well as a reading for Alfred Hitchcock, and was signed to a seven-year contract with no screen test! "Mine was a rare and wonderful Cinderella story that could only have happened during the studio system era," Rhonda recalls. The camera loved Rhonda and her flaming red hair, and for her first substantial role she was cast as a nymphomaniac in the thriller *Spellbound*. "What is a nymphomaniac?" she asked. "I was horrified when I looked it up in the dictionary. At least it wasn't typecasting." Some of her scenes were left on the cutting room floor in the final cut because they felt her performance took away from the star, Ingrid Bergman.

Rhonda went on to co-star with Bing Crosby in the musical *A Connecticut Yankee in King Arthur's Court*, also *Gunfight at the O.K. Corral* with Burt Lancaster and Kirk Douglas and *The Big Circus* with Victor Mature and Vincent Price, among many others. In all, she's made over forty-eight motion pictures and movies for television and starred on Broadway, Las Vegas and a one-woman concert at the Hollywood Bowl.

In between picture commitments, Rhonda took her talent on the road as part of a traveling gospel quartet called The Four Girls, with Jane Russell, Connie Haines and Beryl Davis. They made an album that sold over a million copies and Rhonda recorded her own CD presenting her beautiful singing voice, titled *Rhonda Fleming Sings Just For You*.

Rhonda's middle name should be "Charity." These days she spends an enormous amount of her time, talent and resources touching people in a positive, uplifting way. Through her generosity, a chapel on a huge ranch near Palm Springs was built for the children of Childhelp, USA, which exists to meet the needs of abused children, and over the door a sign reads, "All Who Enter Here Will Find Love."

Fleming is most proud of the non-profit organization PATH (People Assisting the Homeless), whose mission is to break the cycle of homelessness by helping people to become self-sufficient, and where she created the Rhonda Fleming Family Center for homeless women and children. After losing her sister to ovarian cancer, Rhonda and then-husband Ted Mann (Mann Theatres) established the Rhonda Fleming Mann Clinic for Women's Comprehensive Care at UCLA Medical Center and the Rhonda Fleming Mann Research Fellowship at the City of Hope for research on women's cancer.

"I'm grateful and blessed," she says, "for knowing the Lord, my good health and my precious family. I'm gratified to be able to use what name value I have to help people, to touch them in a positive way." These days Rhonda performs only for charity events and her two stars, the other on the Hollywood Walk of Fame, and numerous awards and citations seem hardly enough thanks to a lady who is all about helping people…but it's a start!

For more information or to purchase her CD, go to Rhonda's website at *rhondafleming.com*.

Ruth Gibson does a dance on her star.

EGADS...SHE'S 91!
RUTH GIBSON

STAR #177
DEDICATED JANUARY 24, 2000
265 S. PALM CANYON DR.

Ruth Gibson is one of those unique individuals always full of music, laughter and life and where she likes to live it is Palm Springs, California.

She found what she loves early in life. At just five years old, in her hometown of Greensboro, North Carolina, with ukulele in hand, she sat at the piano, feet not reaching the pedals, and sang to whoever would listen. "I inherited my mother's talent and winning personality," Ruth says. She and Mom sang in a church quartet for funerals; only, when everyone else was crying, Ruth was giggling...and still does. When competing in an amateur talent show, and leading a singing group not quite up to her standards, she turned to the audience and shouted out, "Can you believe this group?!" She won in the Best Comedy category!

During high school, and on the road with her dearly-loved brother, she sang with the Barney Rapp seventeen-piece big band. A brother-and-sister act, he sang/emceed and "played the bass...badly," she says. "I wrote all his material." She also wrote, directed and starred in a high-school musical production. With no formal training, Ruth wrote for Tony Pastor and Stan Kenton, who took several of her songs on the road with him.

Gibson married young and involved herself in another production: three kids, two of them twins. She moved her family to Orlando, continued her career while raising them and, as the breadwinner of the family, worked three simultaneous jobs: account executive of a national advertising agency, nightclub singer and radio station DJ. "I made $125 a week and couldn't spend it all," she says.

After her divorce, Ruth met and married Dana Gibson, who she describes as "the love of my life," and moved to Cocoa Beach, Florida, where she hosted, and wrote the theme song, for a late night talk radio show, *Top of the Stairs*, which was broadcast from the club of the same name. Then the inevitable happened...Ruth and two of her indomitable girlfriends bought a club which they called The Pillow Talk Lounge. It was the hippest, happening place to be and the hangout for astronauts and the mayor. So now, Ms. Go-Getter was a nightclub performer/manager, a publicist and a writer for the local newspaper.

Ruth and me at our shared birthday party.

In spite of all this success, Mr. & Mrs. Gibson moved to Los Angeles. They settled in Marina Del Rey where she found all the great jazz music and began booking musicians in various clubs. The happy couple purchased a 52' boat, the *Tickie 2*, which later sank– taking three thousand copies of her music down with it!

Somewhere along the way, Ruth and her entourage discovered Palm Springs, started making frequent trips to the beautiful desert, and before long took up residence. "I thought I died and went to heaven," she quipped. "There was even more music happening there! I met the late, great piano players Joe Masters and Andy Fraga at the Club Trinidad, and met desert stars Pat Rizzo and Mike Costley at the Club Ocotillo." Pat Rizzo says this about Ruth: "I love her dearly. A great writer and a great person, she shoots from the hip, just like Hoot Gibson. And she never loses her hat!" Mike Costley says, "She writes clever lyrics and wrote a song for me called 'There's Magic in Michael's Music.' She's supportive of all musicians, always on our side."

When her beloved husband passed away, Ruth got seriously into the talent agency business, forming Ruth Gibson Reps and booked musicians all over town. She was hired as senior editor for *Sand to Sea Magazine* and freelanced an entertainment column for *The Desert Sun* newspaper as well. Her love of music led her to establish the Jazz Appreciation Music Society (JAMS), an acronym she cleverly thought up. She's written a staggering number of songs, including the most-requested "Swinging Piano Bar" and "Swing into Spring." Not to mention the parodies "Telephone Man," "Rancho Mirage," "Palm Desert," "La Quinta," and many others.

All of Ruth's countless friends were invited to Vicky's restaurant on January 25, 2010, as we celebrated her annual "surprise" birthday party, and that year...egads, she became a nonagenarian!

The Walk of Stars loves Ruth Gibson and the feeling is mutual and her shining star will always be there to remind us. Keep on swingin', baby!

Buddy Greco and Lezlie Anders at their nightclub, Greco's.

TWO SHINING STARS

BUDDY GRECO & LEZLIE ANDERS

STAR #304
DEDICATED FEBRUARY 13, 2008
538 N. PALM CANYON DR.

A distinguished couple on and off the stage, Buddy Greco and Lezlie Anders have been entertaining delighted audiences for many years. Buddy began performing professionally with his dad in their hometown of Philadelphia at five years old, first singing and acting and then playing piano. In his teenage years he formed a trio and worked in local nightclubs where he met Benny Goodman's manager and joined the great Benny Goodman big band, as an arranger as well as a performer. Later, Greco went out on his own, entertaining in theatres and clubs all over the world, including a performance with the Beatles for the Queen of England. He has recorded sixty-eight albums and sold records in the millions, ranging in style from jazz to country to pop. Greco is known for such hits as "The Lady Is a Tramp," "Around the World" and "MacArthur Park." He's been inducted into the Philadelphia Music Alliance's Walk of Fame and is listed in numerous Who's Who in music books, including the *Encyclopedias of Great Jazz Singers and Musicians.*

The multi-talented Lezlie Anders began her career in business, as a divestiture specialist and broker. Among her holdings was a nightclub in Oregon, where she began singing while earning a degree in music. She formed a big band and hosted a popular talk/music radio show. Later,

Lezlie moved to Las Vegas to perform at the Desert Inn, as well as other main hotels.

Lezlie and Buddy met while they were working in Las Vegas. After performing in the desert area many times, including shows with my husband, musician Whitey Mitchell, they moved to Palm Desert where they entertained pleased desert dwellers and visitors for three years at their successful nightclub, aptly named Buddy Greco's Supper Club. They toured Europe, performing in England, Scotland, Ireland and France, with their drummer, Buddy Greco, Jr., and bass player Danny Flahive. Their shows were so successful and lucrative they picked up and moved there!

The Grecos produced the critically acclaimed stage show entitled *Fever! The Music of Peggy Lee*, which premiered in London's West End in 2010.

As the first couple of Palm Springs entertainment, Buddy and Lezlie Greco's star, hosted by friends and fellow star recipients, Chuck & Gayle Hodges and Janie Hughes, continues to shine.

Gloria Greer

A STAR WITH HER PALS
GLORIA GREER

STAR #102
DEDICATED OCTOBER 31, 1997
123 NO. PALM CANYON DRIVE

Living in Beverly Hills, and not exactly down and out, Gloria Greer attended Beverly Hills High School and wrote an entertainment column for a local publication, *The Beverly Hills Bulletin*, as well as a story for *The Hollywood Reporter* on being the daughter of celebrities. This she could do from a realistic point of view because Gloria was indeed part of a celebrity family…Mom was a writer who founded *Sand To Sea Magazine* and Dad was Broadway producer and composer Anatole Friedland. Her stepdad was prolific television and film director Lew Landers, who had literally hundreds of credits, including the Emmy-nominated *Topper* series, *Bat Masterson* and *Maverick*. Additionally, Gloria had several aunts and uncles who were noted editors and journalists.

After high school, Gloria studied psychiatry at UCLA (which may be why she's such a good interviewer). She became a regular on the popular radio serial *Guiding Light*, the longest-running soap opera in radio and TV history, and later appeared on the television shows *Dr. Christian* with Macdonald Carey and *Highway Patrol* with Broderick Crawford. While she thought about being an actress, Gloria's career took a different direction when she accepted a job as columnist for the daily and weekly *Variety* trade paper which led to a position as correspondent for *Newsweek* magazine, which led a writing job for the Pulitzer Prize-winning paper *The Press-Enterprise*. "I got that job," she says, "after I wrote about Frank

Sinatra, Desi Arnaz and Robert Stack who had a heated argument at Desi's Indian Wells estate regarding the series *The Untouchables*. It was the front page on the wire stories and was picked up by *The Desert Sun* and *The Press Enterprise*. So I called the *Enterprise* and told them that story started with me and they ought to have me writing for them."

Gloria was editor and publisher of *Sand To Sea Magazine* and sold it in 1999 to *Palm Springs Life Magazine* where it appears as a special edition titled *The Social Life*. In addition, this dynamic lady hosts and produces three different television shows simultaneously! Her show *Conversations with Gloria Greer*, on Time Warner Cable TV, is broadcast four times a week; *Classic Conversations with Gloria Greer* on KVCR-TV revisits her special interviews of the past thirty-five years; *Exploring the Arts* is an in-depth look at the visual and performing arts. Her guests have included such luminaries as Presidents Reagan and Ford, Walter Cronkite, Walter Annenberg, Prime Minister Benjamin Netanyahu, Brad Pitt, Sophia Loren, Ginger Rogers, and Liberace.

Greer has been inducted into the Academy of Television Arts & Sciences prestigious Silver Circle, received the Athena Award from the Palm Springs Chamber of Commerce and been named Press Woman of the Year by my own organization, the Palm Springs Women's Press Club. She serves on the boards of the Air Museum and Women in Film & Television. After one of Gloria's twin daughters was diagnosed with Multiple Sclerosis, she founded ACT for MS, an organization offering physical, educational and financial assistance to those afflicted with this incurable disease. Gloria is constantly in demand to attend events such as the women's advocacy group World of Women (WOW) luncheons and as a celebrity guest on cruise ships. Five percent of cruise fees have been donated to ACT for MS.

Gloria tirelessly continues her community service in so many other areas. "I believe success is measured by how we help those less fortunate," she says, "and an appreciation of the performing and visual arts enriches all our lives." Her well-deserved star is in good company near some of her pals, Dolores Hope, Frederick Loewe and Frank Sinatra.

Gloria's star party was hosted by friend, and star recipient, local philanthropist Jackie Lee Houston and since it happened to be October 31, some people came in costume. That was the start of the Houstons' illustrious annual Houston Halloween parties.

Mel Haber at the bar of his restaurant, Melvyn's, at the Ingleside Inn.

THERE'S STILL ROOM AT THE INN!
MEL HABER

STAR #70
DEDICATED OCTOBER 23, 1996
123 N. PALM CANYON DR.

Only in America could a skinny kid from Brooklyn named Melvyn wind up in Palm Springs, California, the playground of the stars, hosting everyone from peasants to presidents.

The son of a garment district salesman, Haber sold raccoon tails during the Davy Crockett phase and, not one to take a backseat to anyone, later became a successful manufacturer of those popular gyrating auto dashboard hula dolls and other automotive accessories. He came to California from New York as a vacationer, spotted the historic Ingleside Inn in Palm Springs, fell in love and made an offer on it within fifteen minutes. After extensive renovations to the property and adding a restaurant, he opened Melvyn's Ingleside Inn, which has become one of the ten best destination resorts, according to *Lifestyles of the Rich & Famous*. Some of the most celebrated people on the planet have stayed at the Inn, including Marlon Brando, Clark Gable, Cher, Frank Sinatra, Elizabeth Taylor and John Travolta.

But Haber didn't stop there. In 1979 he opened the upscale Cecil's Disco (where he met his beautiful wife, Stephanie), followed by a club he called Saturdays and after that, one called Doubles. He had four thriving venues going at once and worked seven days a week, personally supervising every club, every night. In the early '80s, Mel was the largest employer in the city of Palm Springs. By the '90s, these clubs were sold and he opened yet another nightspot, an elegant disco, called Touché, which catered to the beautiful people. But before long it too was sold, and he turned all his attention to Melvyn's Ingleside Inn. "AIDS and MADD (Mothers Against Drunk Driving) killed the disco business," Mel recalls. "I learned that concentration is the key to economic success…stick to one instead of opening four or five places."

Enjoying all this success, Mel began to wonder, "How can I do some good…give something back?" And the answer came in the form of Angel View Crippled Children's Foundation. He held Sunday dances for teenagers and kids from Angel View. They were bused in, and they would dance from their wheelchairs. He was so moved by being able to bring some happiness to these children that he joined the board of Angel View and later became president. "In twenty-nine years, I've missed only one meeting," he proudly reports. "More than half of my calls every day are regarding Angel View. After I'm gone, it might not get me upstairs, but hopefully it'll slow my descent downstairs!"

Mel enjoys speaking engagements and will squeeze one in for the asking. He's been guest speaker for Brandeis University, Temple Isaiah, my own group, the Palm Springs Women's Press Club, and others. He has published two books, *Bedtime Stories*, tales of his experiences at the Inn, and *Palm Springs a la Carte, the Colorful world of the Caviar Crowd*. Both are available at Amazon.com or InglesideInn.com.

Every new season, Haber hosts the successful *Dinner With* series, a variety of noted authors, actors, politicians, screenwriters, etc., who share their latest books and experiences. Past speakers have been prolific writer Andrew Neiderman, musician extraordinaire Bill Marx, the late Tony Curtis and my dear late husband, screenwriter-producer-musician Gordon "Whitey" Mitchell.

Mel Haber received his richly deserved star on his 60th birthday and that same year the city made the Ingleside Inn an official historic site. And, yes, there is still room at the Inn!

Monty Hall.

LET'S MAKE A DEAL!
MONTY HALL

STAR #79
DEDICATED DECEMBER 14, 1996
123 NO. PALM CANYON DR.

Wanna make a deal? Game show legend Monty Hall made a deal with CBS to be the consultant for a new *Let's Make A Deal*, starring popular talk show host, actor, singer and Emmy winner Wayne Brady as host.

Born in Winnipeg, Canada, Maurice Halperin studied at the University of Manitoba, was elected President of the Student Body, was recruited to do a dramatic radio show and became active as a singer, emcee, sportscaster and actor in the college productions. Moving to Toronto to pursue his show-business career, he landed a television show on the CBC called *Floor Show*, which led to an NBC program in New York called *Monitor*. After that five-year run, Hall relocated to Hollywood to emcee a CBS game show, *Video Village*, which ran for two years. During that time, Monty met and teamed up with writer/producer Stefan Hatos, forming Hatos-Hall Productions to create the high-energy game show *Let's Make A Deal*.

Monty says the outrageous costumes on the show came about by accident. "People first came in normal clothes," he said. "I picked people at random. One day a woman in the audience came with a sign: 'Roses are red, violets are blue. I came here to DEAL with you!' So I picked her. Next thing I knew, everyone had a sign. Next came wild and crazy hats. Then came five hundred people all dressed up for Halloween!" He says the best prize ever given away was His & Her Cadillacs and the worst, called "zonks," were clunker cars, goats, pigs or cows. He would give cash prizes to anyone who had the strange items he asked for. Monty has done 4,178 performances in twenty-seven years and *Let's Make A Deal* is licensed in fourteen countries throughout the world.

"When I'm out in public, he says, "I'm frequently accosted by someone who says, 'I'll give you $100 for a hard-boiled egg,' or if I'm getting into an elevator, somebody will always ask, 'Do you want Door #1, 2 or 3?'" One night in a restaurant bar, while waiting for his table, the bartender approached Monty offering to buy drinks for his party if he had a paper clip on him. Well, he did have one in an envelope in his pocket and also had a large dinner party of eight!

Hall has guest-starred on television shows such as *Love, American Style*, *Laugh-In* and *The Odd Couple*, and headlined at the Sarah Hotel in Las Vegas, where he sang, danced and did comedy, but says he didn't much enjoy it. "I didn't like living in a dressing room." Now he sings at parties only.

Well known for his humanitarian efforts, Monty Hall has raised over one billion dollars for charity. Variety Clubs International created a lifetime position for him as International Chairman. He has generously donated so much of his time and energy to fundraising that he's collected more than five hundred honors and awards worldwide, including hospital wings named after him, and was the former Honorary Mayor of Hollywood (before Johnny Grant). He has been given the Order of Canada and the Order of Manitoba, that country's highest civilian honors, and he was given the first-ever Icon Award from the Game Show Network. His star shines in three locations…one on the Hollywood Walk of Fame, one on the Palm Springs Walk of Stars and one in Canada's Walk of Fame in Toronto. And you can stroll down Monty Hall Drive in Cathedral City, California, or Monty Hall Street in Winnipeg, Canada. "It's the same street," he says. "It goes all the way from Highway 111 in the desert to Winnipeg."

The talented Hall family is more like a dynasty. Monty's wife, Marilyn, is an Emmy Award-winning producer who has produced an independent feature, *The Little Traitor*, for Regent Films. Daughter Joanna Gleason won the Tony Award as Best Actress (Musical) for *Into the Woods*. Son Richard is a reality show producer and daughter Sharon is an executive producer at Sony Pictures.

It's been a long, wonderful journey from Canada to Hollywood, Beverly Hills and Palm Springs, California, and we're glad the Halperin family made the trip!

Denise DuBarry Hay on star day with her daughter and mother.

ASK A BUSY PERSON
DENISE DuBARRY HAY

STAR #222
DEDICATED MAY 10, 2002
310 N. PALM CANYON DRIVE

They say if you want something done, ask a busy person. I asked...and Denise DuBarry Hay found time to tell me about her acting, producing, entrepreneurial and humanitarian projects.

As a painfully shy young girl, she joined a friend in acting classes and says, "I created my own world with the other actors and forgot about the camera." Bitten by the acting bug, Denise got lucky early and starred in numerous commercials, and made a screen test with Sylvester Stallone, as well as for Steven Spielberg, later learning she was Spielberg's second choice for a role that eventually went to Kate Capshaw, whom he later married.

Next came roles in *Days of our Lives*, *The Love Boat*, *Charlie's Angels*, *CHiPs* and many others. She played opposite Palm Springs' former mayor and U.S. Congressman the late Sonny Bono in a movie for television, entitled *Top of the Hill*. Denise may best be known for her role in TV's *Black Sheep Squadron* with Robert Conrad, as well as the 1979 Oscar-nominated film *Being There*, with Peter Sellers and Shirley MacLaine.

While continuing her acting career, Denise founded a production company and produced a "how-to" video, *Play the Piano Overnight*. She became a pioneer and creative icon in a new marketing medium, the infomercial industry. With husband Bill Hay, Denise created Thane International, a direct marketing company, distributing over ninety products worldwide, which have generated over $1 billion in sales.

In 2005, Denise and Bill sold Thane and founded Kaswit, Inc., an acronym for her kids' names. A few of Kaswit's direct response products are The Pilates Power Gym, which sells on the Home Shopping Network; The Stash 'n Dash Sash, a pocketed hands-free scarf; and the DVD *Secrets to Training the Perfect Dog*.

Through her film production company, Blue Moxie Entertainment, Denise produced the action-comedy feature *Shoot the Hero*, which premiered at the International Film Festival. The film, which aired on Showtime, stars daughter Samantha Lockwood, Jason Mewes and local favorite Fred (The Hammer) Williamson. It's available at Amazon.com and Netflix. A project currently in development is *Friends with Secrets*, based on a book she optioned titled *Husbands Come and Go, But Friends Are Forever*.

Over thirty years ago Denise discovered the rejuvenating benefits of yoga, and still practices every day. She became a certified yoga instructor and with partner Kim Tang, recently opened a new studio, Bikram Yoga University Village, in Palm Desert, California. "This yoga studio is the best within a hundred miles," she boasts. "The benefits of yoga are huge… lowers blood pressure, cures chronic ailments such as arthritis, diabetes, weight issues and revitalizes tissues." To learn more, go to bikramyogauvpalmdesert.com.

As a founding member and past president of Women in Film & Television, Denise still serves on the board and helped increase the membership by 400%, developed their programs and website and was presented with their Diva of the Desert Award for 2010. *Palm Springs Life* magazine named her one of the top twenty most dynamic women. Denise was formerly on the board of the Palm Springs International Film Festival and now serves on the board at Marywood-Palm Valley private school in Rancho Mirage, California.

Denise DuBarry Hay devotes much of her time, talent and resources to Olive Crest, an organization dedicated to helping abused children. She transformed the lives of hundreds of abused children by tirelessly helping build four safe homes.

Her long-time pal, the late producer, humanitarian and former Chairman of the Palm Springs International Film Festival, Earl Greenburg sponsored Denise's well-deserved star. You can tell this is one busy and beautiful lady who makes things happen rather than waiting for things to come to her.

Herb Jeffries on interview day.

THE BRONZE BUCKAROO
HERB JEFFRIES

STAR #135
DEDICATED JANUARY 20, 1998
275 SO. PALM CANYON DRIVE

He became a singer, actor, director, producer, and writer, but people first heard Umberto Ballentino, aka Herb Jeffries, singing on the streets of a mixed neighborhood in the Detroit ghetto where they dropped coins in a bucket for him. Herb was born to an Irish mother and a Sicilian father he never met. Mom ran a boarding house for musicians and his stepdad introduced him to jazz. Growing up, Herb sang in the house, in the church choir and in restaurants for tips, when he wasn't at the movies watching Westerns. "You could get in for 10 or 15 cents," he said. "I'd stay all day wondering how those actors got on that screen."

As a young adult, Jeffries answered an ad for a singer with a jazz band. In those days, jazz was only played by "colored" or "Negro" bands and when asked his nationality, Herb, too dark to be white and too white to be black, answered, "Creole…from New Orleans. I didn't care if it was a Chinese band. I just wanted to sing that kind of music!" He got the gig singing with the Erskine Tate jazz band at the Savoy Ballroom in Chicago for $5 a night. Before long, piano man Earl "Fatha" Hines offered Herb more money to go on the road as the vocalist with his band. When they appeared in the South, it was Herb's first direct encounter with racial discrimination. At segregated movie theatres he would see crowds of Negros waiting to get in to see the white cowboys. There were no African-American heroes or role models and he vowed to change all that.

In his twenties, Jeffries set out for Hollywood and managed to contact a producer, pitched him the notion of making a series of Westerns featuring an all-black cast. The first picture released was *Harlem on the Prairie* starring Jeffries, who was the first actor ever to portray an African-American hero in the first-ever African-American cowboy film. He went on to make four of these so-called "race films," including *The Bronze Buckaroo*.

While on the road making personal appearances to promote his movies, Herb met the distinguished American composer and orchestra leader Duke Ellington, who asked him to tour with his band. Duke, a very articulate man, sent Herb to singer Dick Haymes' mother, a voice teacher, for elocution lessons. Herb was the first male singer to work with Ellington and is the last living survivor of the band. "He's the most wonderful man I've ever met," said Jeffries, who became identified with such standards as "Satin Doll," "Sophisticated Lady" and his signature song "Flamingo," which sold over fourteen million records worldwide. Known as "Mr. Flamingo," Herb likes to quip, "Most people come into this world by stork…I came by Flamingo and Duke Ellington delivered me!" Years later he recorded a tribute CD entitled *The Duke and I*, honoring the great musician's 100th birthday.

Herb travelled throughout Europe as an entertainer and later as a draftee during World War II, and in France he saw no racial bigotry. "Whatever nationality you were, you were treated the same," he said, and knew he'd return someday. Back in the States, Herb went to Las Vegas to headline at the major hotels, but again faced discrimination; he wasn't allowed to stay where he performed. He moved his family to Paris and opened two successful nightclubs, which quickly became hangouts for royalty and the jet-set crowd. After ten years Herb grew tired of the demands on a club owner/performer and relocated to the U.S. in the '60s, returning to movies, recordings and now television. He guested on hit shows such as *Hawaii Five-O*, *The Virginian* and *I Dream of Jeannie*. He appeared in the motion picture *Calypso Joe* with Angie Dickinson and later wrote and directed the film *Mundo Depravados*, starring his then-wife, burlesque queen Tempest Storm, which became a cult classic.

Besides being acknowledged with two stars, one on the Hollywood Walk of Fame, Herb has been inducted into the Western Performers Hall of Fame at the National Cowboy & Western Heritage Museum, received the Golden Boot Award from the Motion Picture & Television Fund and earned the Cowboy Spirit Award from the Festival of the West. In 2005 the city of Palm Desert paid tribute to him by dedicating The Herb Jeffries Trail.

The legendary Herb Jeffries, the Bronze Buckaroo, has done it all...he's performed in every country in the world, sang for a number of kings and for Presidents Truman, Nixon, Ford, Clinton and Bush. In 2003, while performing in the East Room at a White House event celebrating Black Music Month, he was stopped by a man who said he'd been following Herb's career all his life and added, "You're my hero!" That man was the former Secretary of State, General Colin Powell.

These days Herb spends every joyful moment with wife Savannah and says, "She's the best friend I ever had in my life. I adore her and I'm happier than I've ever been!" Herb is working on his autobiography, *The Color of Love*, and says the best is yet to come!

Jack Jones on stage.

THE LOVE BOAT GUY
JACK JONES

STAR #234
DEDICATED APRIL 4, 2003
155 SO. PALM CANYON DR.

How could he not be in show business? His real name is John Allan Jones and he was born on the night his father, singer-actor Allan Jones, recorded his big hit "The Donkey Serenade." Jack attended high school in West Los Angeles and studied drama and singing. Jack's father started his son's show-business career in his teenage years, bringing him on stage in Las Vegas as part of his act. When Jack went out on his own, he played in small clubs and worked on his style which was influenced by Tony Bennett, Frank Sinatra and Mel Tormé. Sinatra described Jones as "One of the major singers of our time" and Mel Tormé referred to him as "The greatest 'pure' singer in the world."

While waiting for his first album to be released and his career to take off, Jack worked at a gas station and as he was cleaning a car windshield, he heard the first of his hit records, "Got a Lot of Livin' to Do," on a customer's radio. In 1959 Jack recorded an album and a few singles for Capitol Records, but was dropped by the label. He found better luck with Kapp Records when he recorded his hit single "Lollipops and Roses," which was followed by another hit, "Wives and Lovers," each recording earning him a highly-coveted Grammy Award for Best Male Vocal Performance. Jones has recorded many television themes, the best known being for *The Love Boat*, and he tells this story: "At every cruise I went on they'd play my record. Everyone would stand on the dock throwing confetti and singing 'The Love Boat.' I went out on the dock one day incognito and stood there to see if anyone would notice it was me. I started to sing along and somebody told me to shut up because they couldn't hear Jack Jones singing!"

In show business for more than fifty-three years, Jack has recorded over fifty albums, seventeen of which have been in *Billboard* magazine's top twenty hits. He's appeared on numerous television shows and movies, performed countless concerts all over the world, from nightclubs to the London Palladium, appeared at the White House, Carnegie Hall, the Kennedy Center and plays to consistently sold-out audiences everywhere. His legitimate stage roles include *Guys and Dolls*, *South Pacific* and *Man of La Mancha*. Perennial favorite Jack Jones has two stars…the other one on the Hollywood Walk of Fame, right next to Dad.

Dorothy Dale Kloss on stage at the Follies.

THE WORLD'S OLDEST SHOWGIRL!
DOROTHY DALE KLOSS

STAR #330
DEDICATED MAY 29, 2010
128 SO. PALM CANYON DR.

Everything old is new again. So it seemed to me, listening to Dorothy Dale Kloss, at 87, talk about her passion for performing and her still-a-work-in-progress life. She began dancing at age three, when most of us couldn't even tie our own shoelaces. Born and raised in Chicago, Dorothy's supportive mother, a beauty shop owner, stretched her budget to give her daughter dance lessons. Dorothy won the contests and, in her teenage years, progressed to become an instructor herself. Among her classmates were the legendary dancers Bob Fosse and June Taylor. It was a time when Jazz and Swing were a part of America's mainstream music. What's more, she taught Bob Fosse (*All That Jazz*) how to dance!

By age fourteen, Dorothy moved on to become a dancer at the Empire Room of the famed Palmer House Hotel, appearing onstage at 10pm (before child labor laws were in effect), and, while still in high school, became the featured act at the historic hotel's main showroom. Dorothy now had developed into one of the famous Merriel Abbott Dancers, Chicago's answer to New York City's Rockettes. "I quickly realized I needed to purchase orchestrations, costumes and shoes," Dorothy recalls. "I approached Miss Abbott, who asked me if I think I'm sprinkled with stardust and based on my enthusiastic 'yes,' she just gave them to me, saying, 'Go knock 'em dead!'"

When the popular bandleader Eddy Duchin came to the Palmer House, Dorothy became the featured dancer and went on tour with the band, always sending money back home to Mom. Later, she traveled with big band greats Ray Noble, Skinnay Ennis and Shep Fields & His Rippling Rhythm. "Shep's rhythm wasn't all that rippled," Dorothy reveals. "His hands would ripple right to me and I had to slap him!" No word on whether or not she lost that gig.

In 1940 Dorothy was asked to work with Cantinflas and found her-

Dorothy at her star party with Charlie Chaplin look-alike, Audrey Ruttan.

self doing two shows a day for a year at the trendy El Patio nightspot in Mexico City, with an occasional audience like Clark Gable, Carole Lombard, Charlie Chaplin and Gloria Swanson. Right about here, if I didn't already know, I'd be asking, "Just how old are you, anyway?" One night, while doing the time step, Pearl Harbor was bombed and the show closed.

Back in Chicago, Dorothy secured her own radio show and was the first person to tap dance on television. She signed with an agent who sent her on the road again, and while busy with stints at the Chez Paree and the Copacabana, still made time to entertain the troops at USOs and naval stations.

Fast forward to the fifties; Dorothy married, produced a son, Craig, and took time off to raise him. Some years later, Dorothy suffered the loss of her beloved mother and says, "Memories of her are my most treasured possession. She's the person I hope I've become." Now divorced, Dorothy took Craig to the West Coast. Sometime in the eighties she overcame a bout with colon cancer and has been cancer-free ever since.

It was while teaching dance at the Pasadena Senior Center when one of her students suggested she check out the *Palm Springs Follies*. "I made a video, went to the *Follies* audition in Hollywood and was told to hang by the phone that weekend." She got the call and moved to Palm Springs.

Dorothy, now retired, had maintained a grueling schedule doing nine three-hour shows a week, from October thru May each year. She was at the theatre from 12:30 to 10:15 at night. I asked how difficult that was: "It's like rolling off a log. It's the boredom backstage waiting to go on." In between acts, Dorothy made notes for her forthcoming book titled *Still Clicking My Heels at 86, 87, 88…Love, Dorothy*.

Her all-time favorite performer to work with is Kaye Ballard, who was one of the speakers on star day, as well as Rita Coolidge and longtime roommate Ken Prescott, whom she met in the show years ago. Ken, previously a singer with The Modernaires and former star of Broadway's *42nd Street*, says of Dorothy, "I've never met someone with so much talent, who is so honest and straight on and never has a mean agenda towards anyone."

The Guinness Book of World Records lists Dorothy as "The oldest performing showgirl in the world." On January 15, 2009, Mayor Steve Pougnet declared it to be "Dorothy Dale Kloss Day" and on May 29, 2010, she received the distinction of being only the second *Follies* performer to receive a star on the Walk of Stars, thereby giving her two Dorothy Day Kloss Days.

It's only fitting that her star will shine forever at the front entrance of the fabulous *Palm Springs Follies*! Dorothy's star day was sponsored by her good pals Lisette and Boyd Haigler.

Ruta Lee on stage with Senior Class.

THE POT AT THE END OF THE RAINBOW
RUTA LEE

STAR #40
DEDICATED JANUARY 15, 1995
455 N. PALM CANYON DR.

Canadian-born Ruta Lee, daughter of an immigrant Lithuanian tailor, began her show-business career while still in high school, working as an usher and then a candy girl at the famed Grauman's Chinese Theatre in Hollywood. She was promoted to box-office cashier, but then was quickly fired...her dancing was better than her math! After graduation, Ruta Mary Kilmonis found work in the movie *Seven Brides for Seven Brothers*, followed by *Anything Goes*, *Witness for the Prosecution* and as Frank Sinatra's leading lady in *Sergeants 3*. She's appeared in over two hundred television shows, including, *The Lucy Show*, *The Love Boat*, *Love, American Style*, *The Twilight Zone* and *Hawaiian Eye*.

This multi-talented lady has headlined in musicals all over the country, in such shows as *Hello, Dolly!*, *Mame*, *Woman of the Year* and *Best Little Whorehouse in Texas*. She was a regular on TV's *Hollywood Squares* and *What's My Line?*, and starred in three Hallmark made-for-TV Christmas specials which air every holiday season: *A Christmas Too Many* with Mickey Rooney, *Love's Pure Light* and *Christmas At Cadillac Jack's*. In the desert, Lee co-starred in the hit musical revue *Senior Class*, the highly amusing play celebrating life's golden years, which first appeared at the Palm d'Or Theatre and then relocated to the Annenberg Theatre in Palm Springs.

In 1964, Lee made international headlines when she managed to call then-Soviet leader Nikita Khrushchev and convince him to release her ninety-year-old grandmother from an internment camp in Siberia. Ruta brought Grandma to the United States to live out her days with her.

Ruta spends a great deal of time and energy on charities, her favorite being The Thailians. She says, "There isn't one benefit they don't call me for." She's chairman and founder, along with Debbie Reynolds, of the organization that benefits mentally disabled people through the Thailians

Ruta on star day.

Community Mental Health Center at Cedars-Sinai Medical Center in Los Angeles. Ruta co-chairs the fundraising galas in Beverly Hills and has done so for over forty-seven years. Honorees have been Clint Eastwood, Frank Sinatra, Sammy Davis, Jr., and Bob Hope. "When not performing," she says, "I spend most of my time working to make life more wonderful for those who need help through my charitable endeavors and contributions." And for these efforts, Ruta has received the prestigious Yellow Rose of Texas Award from President George W. Bush as well as the City of Hope's Spirit of Life Award, among others. In New York City, Lee emceed and entertained at the Culinary Institute of America (CIA) Leadership Awards. The group celebrates the best and brightest of the food service industry.

A two-star gal, her Palm Springs star sits in front of the Blue Coyote Mexican restaurant and she notes, "JFK has an eternal flame…I have an eternal marguerita!" But it was her dream to have a star in Hollywood and in 2006 her lifelong dream was fulfilled when she received a star on Hollywood Boulevard right smack in front of her former employer, the historic Grauman's Chinese Theatre. She calls it "the pot at the end of the rainbow."

Ruta is married to Texas restaurant executive Webb Lowe and the busy couple divides their time between homes in Hollywood, Palm Springs, Fort Worth, and Las Hadas, Mexico. "I sleep around," she jokes!

Rich Little.

MAKING A GOOD IMPRESSION

RICH LITTLE

STAR #134
DEDICATED NOVEMBER 14, 1998
275 S. PALM CANYON DR.

Canadian-born Rich Little was a veteran impressionist in his teenage years. "I was always fascinated with people's lives and interested in human behavior. I imitated their walks," he says. "I got laughs when I answered the teacher's questions with impressions of their own voices. It was a way to be popular."

On stage, and paid to do his impressions since age seventeen, Rich was discovered in the U.S. by his friend, jazz singer Mel Tormé, who brought him to *The Judy Garland Show*. Little followed that up with appearances on the Ed Sullivan, Jackie Gleason and Dean Martin variety shows. He continued with his uncanny ability to become someone else on his own show in the '70s, hosted Johnny Carson's *Tonight Show* twelve times and starred in the television show *KopyKat*s. He's done HBO specials, sitcoms and recorded over nine albums.

Dubbed the "Man of a Thousand Voices," Rich Little's spot-on impressions include Johnny Carson, Jimmy Stewart, John Wayne (he taught Rich how to do his walk), Jack Benny, Frank Sinatra, Humphrey Bogart, Dr. Phil, Stallone, Nicholson, Schwarzenegger, Eastwood and all ten presidents from JFK to Obama. His repertoire contains well over 200 celebrities. I asked which personality he relates to most: "My favorite, by far, is Ronald Reagan. I can really get into his character. I think I also do Johnny Carson and Jay Leno the best." The most difficult: "The ones I can't do, the current film superstars…Matt Damon, Brad Pitt and George Clooney."

Rich recalled a past show he did here in Palm Springs: "Bob and Dolores Hope were in the audience, in the front row. Hope couldn't hear well. Dolores repeated the punch lines, yelling in his ear, after every joke. So Bob was the only one always laughing late, right in the middle of the next joke."

Comedy is also a serious business, as when Little was called to do soundtrack re-dubbings for incapacitated stars. He did voices for an ailing David Niven and a deceased Peter Sellers in the *Pink Panther* movies. When Stacey Keach couldn't finish his voice-overs for TV's *Mike Hammer*, Rich stepped in, and when Gene Kelly lost his voice doing a television special, he did him as well.

Little's other passion is his charcoal drawings and he has been sketching since age fourteen. Selections include Frank Sinatra, Cary Grant, Clark Gable and George Burns, among many others. These 8x10 drawings, along with his DVDs, are sold after his shows and on the Internet, and are personally autographed and numbered, with a certificate of authenticity. He says John Wayne outsells all others. To purchase, go to *www.richlittle.com*.

These days, Rich is having fun touring the country with his one-man show, *Jimmy Stewart & Friends*, which he hopes to take to Broadway. It's not only about Stewart; he reaches back to the golden age with "conversations" between Stewart and his many famous movie star friends.

Active in numerous charities, Rich has generously supported the Ottawa Civic Hospital in Ottawa, Canada, and was honored with the establishment of the "Rich Little Special Care Nursery" at the hospital. He has donated his time, talent and resources to Juvenile Diabetes, Children's Miracle Network, the National Kidney Foundation, the Christopher Reeve Paralysis Foundation, the McCallum Theater, the Barbara Sinatra Children's Center and others.

Rich Little richly deserves his four stars…Palm Springs, Los Angeles, Las Vegas and Toronto, Canada. He says he can't really remember exactly where they are all placed, but this past summer, as he was walking on Hollywood Boulevard, someone accidently knocked him down. When he got up, he was standing on his star! I guess there was no one to catch a falling star!

Trini Lopez on star day.

IF HE HAD A HAMMER...
TRINI LOPEZ

STAR #8
DEDICATED MAY 21, 1993
123 N. PALM CANYON DR.

Trini Lopez got his start on the street corners of his hometown of Dallas, Texas, playing a $12 guitar his father managed to buy for him. The famous Gibson guitar has since been inspired by Lopez. Born into a musical but poor family, Trini helped out by singing in clubs throughout the Southwest. At age eighteen he was offered a three-year recording contract and somewhere along the way met and befriended Buddy Holly and his band The Crickets. But fate stepped in when Holly's career was cut short by his death in a plane crash. The band, finding themselves without a leader, asked Trini to join them in Hollywood as their lead singer. A devastated Trini arrived in Hollywood only to learn that the boys in the band weren't ready to go back to a life out on the road. A determined Trini found a solo gig in Beverly Hills' Ye Little Club, which lead to an even better gig at the trendy Hollywood nightclub P.J.'s, where he performed to a packed house for eighteen months.

Frank Sinatra's record producer caught Trini's act, was impressed and brought him to Frank's attention and Trini was signed to Sinatra's Reprise label. His first album for Reprise was *Trini Lopez Live at P.J.'s*, which to this day remains his biggest selling album. Lopez has since recorded 64 albums, including *Ramblin' Man*. He's sold over one hundred million albums worldwide, won many honors, awards and Gold Records and has performed in numerous movies and television shows. Lopez completed a feature role in an independent film shot in the desert called *Palm Springs High School*, in which he performed one of his biggest hits, "La Bamba."

A few years ago, Trini starred in a PBS special, *Trini Lopez Presents Latin Music Legends*, taped at the legendary Orpheum Theatre in Los Angeles. It was produced by Bob Alexander, president of the Walk of Stars, and was written by my beloved late husband, Gordon "Whitey" Mitchell.

Trini with a few of his hit records.

This year, in the Philippines, Trini performed on television, radio and for concerts to over 10,000 delighted fans. He recently recorded an all jazz CD and is currently working on his autobiography.

Trini will always belong to Palm Springs where he plays golf, hosts tournaments and brightens the social and charity scene with his immense talents.

Anita Maltin during a performance.

NAUGHTY BUT NICE!
ANITA MALTIN

STAR #150
DEDICATED MARCH 12, 1999
160 S. PALM CANYON DR.

Anita Maltin started life in London, as the daughter of an upper-class family who ran a candy manufacturing business. She helped out in the family stores while studying journalism in school, but was fascinated with the theatre and became involved in Shakespearean plays. When a talent scout came to the school, she auditioned and, unlike so many stage mothers, her mom hid in a closet. Anita didn't get the part. But she did get a Canadian soldier who took her away to Canada. Unfortunately, he died young and, much later, Anita remarried, a union that lasted over fifty years. When I asked the secret of such a long-term marriage, she hastily replied, "Prozac!"

When her family grew to four, they moved to Los Angeles. Her husband's business took him on the road, while Anita got busy raising the kids, although she did manage to win some small roles in *Traffic Court* and *Divorce Court*. Fast forward eighteen years and it was time to relocate to Palm Springs in retirement. An empty nester now, Anita could pursue her life-long love of show business.

She joined The Valley Players Guild, doing her brand of irreverent humor. Writing her own material, she developed a sassy but classy stand-up routine which became so successful she was able to open her own downtown dinner theatre, The Piccadilly. After three years, Anita closed the club to go it alone and was immediately booked into the historic

Biltmore Hotel, doing her spicy one-woman show. Then came Kilpatrick's nightspot, where she packed the place. "After 11:00pm," she recalls, "I would get the 'naughty crowd.' Nothing really taboo; I would just take them to the edge. For instance: If it weren't for pickpockets, I wouldn't have any sex at all!" I asked what her grandchildren think of her material: "They gave me these jokes!" she shot back!

Maltin's big break came with the opening of a new show in town, the fabulous *Palm Springs Follies*. During open auditions, she performed her routine and sang "I've Got a Lovely Bunch of Cocoanuts" and, glancing over at the show's producer, Riff Markowitz, she saw him nodding approvingly. She got the job and a three consecutive year run. Each night, as she made her grand entrance in an elegant queenly robe, Markowitz would bow to her and say, "Your Grace," and she became known as the Queen of Comedy. "That gig put me on the map," Anita proudly recalls. When it ended, she brought her naughty-but-nice act to the Lawrence Welk Theatre, the Club Trinidad, Moody's Supper Club, and opened for the fabulous Jim Bailey (who impersonates Judy Garland).

While performing at the Rock Garden Café, producer Irwin Rubinsky gathered friends and fans together to present Anita with her star. These days, at age eighty-eight, Anita is still getting bookings. When people ask her to dinner, she accepts with this caveat: "Are you sure? You don't know how much I eat!" She says life is great now. "I turn down more work than I accept. I'm busy with my three dogs, 'Babe,' 'Dolly,' and 'Hillary,'… all Democrats!"

Bill Marx at home with a photo of dad, Harpo Marx, behind him.

SON OF HARPO SPEAKS
BILL MARX

STAR #218
DEDICATED MARCH 23, 2002
265 S. PALM CANYON DR.

"The best advice I ever got," Bill Max recalls, "was from long-time family friend, comedian George Burns, who told me never walk into a room without an opening line." Bill learned his lesson well. He owns every room he enters. And, unlike his father, Harpo Marx, he never holds back from speaking.

Bill studied composition at The Juilliard School and thinks of himself as "a composer who plays the piano, orchestrally." Show business is truly his life. Bill's mom had been an actress on Broadway and in motion pictures, and by age twelve he was on the road with Dad functioning as his personal prop man. "That prop trunk is my most treasured possession," he says. "To this day, everything in it is just the way I packed it after Dad's final performance as Harpo Marx." While still in his teens, Bill began arranging and conducting for his dad's recordings and personal appearances. Later, he made his own recordings and wrote scores for numerous motion pictures and television shows such as *The Love Boat* and *Fantasy Island*. In between assignments, he performed in chic nightclubs all around Los Angeles, but found a home at Dino's Lodge on the famed Sunset Strip where he entertained Hollywood's A-List for five years.

Home now is in California with his supportive and beautiful wife, Barbara, where he's constantly in demand to perform in clubs, at parties and for charity events. He enjoys a huge, enthusiastic following, does speaking engagements, book signings and concerts, in which he sings and tells stories of his life with all those madcap Marxes. "For the most part," he says, "people go through the day without one laugh. If you can make them laugh, it's wonderful."

Always one to want to give something back, Bill and Barbara are on the boards of Act for MS, Angel View and The Virginia Waring International Piano Competition and others. He generously donates his time and talent to perform at the Stroke Recovery Center and says he leaves there with two feet off the ground. "It's the greatest feeling to share a good time with these people. It's a gift you really are giving to yourself and I feel even better than they do." He's working on creating The Harpo Marx Scholarship Foundation and some of the abundant Marx family memorabilia will become part of it.

Mom Susan, Dad Harpo and Son Bill actually have five stars between them. It seems back in the mid-'90s, Harpo's star was dug up and placed in front of Blimpie's hamburger joint on the NW corner of Indian Canyon Dr. Years later, when Mom received her surprise star, it was placed in front of the former Hamburger Hamlet. Then, a few years after that, philanthropists Jim and Jackie Lee Houston presented Bill with his star. Jim Houston arranged to have three new stars installed alongside each other in their present courtyard location, but the two previous Susan Fleming Marx and Harpo Marx stars remain, making that five.

Bill admits that his greatest challenge in life these days is finding a new purpose. "I want to write one more symphonic work," he says. "It's time to see how I've matured and progressed or lapsed into torpor."

The book and audio version of Bill Marx's moving memoir, *Son of Harpo Speaks*, is available at *bearmanormedia.com*.

Dan McGrath and the other Big Boy.

LET'S TALK RADIO
DAN McGRATH

STAR #288
DEDICATED SEPTEMBER 26, 2007
150 S. PALM CANYON DR.

Let's talk radio with radio personality Dan McGrath, whose familiar and welcome voice wakes up and rides to work with the Coachella Valley every day.

"I grew up with music," says Dan. "My dad was an RCA Records executive." His home, in Wheeling, West Virginia, was a virtual house of wax. In grammar school Dan took up the trumpet, learned music theory and played all through college. "It gave me a better understanding of music and an appreciation of what the artists do." In high school, Dan was heard on campus as the DJ of a radio program he started and later studied recording engineering and broadcasting at West Liberty State College in Wheeling. By age 21, he was hanging out at the local radio station and, while off the air, practiced his broadcasting skills. It didn't take long for the station manager to notice that Dan belonged behind the microphone and he put him on the air. "It's where my morning drive experience began. I got to do the thing I still love the most…connect with the people who call in."

In 1984 Dan brought his personality to Music City-USA, aka Nashville, where he worked at several radio and television stations, including broadcasting from the Hard Rock Café. During his Nashville years, McGrath did hundreds of voice-overs and hosted and produced his own television show. But his dream job appeared when he was chosen as the announcer for the Nashville Network's new television program *Prime Time Country*. He got to work alongside the show's producer, Dick Clark. "I have two idols who have inspired me," Dan says; "Dick Clark and Johnny Carson."

Since Dan and his wife, Regina, turned up in beautiful Palm Desert eleven years ago, his station of choice has been the CBS-owned KEZN,

Dan and wife Regina with actor Tony Curtis.

103.1-FM. His top-rated radio show, *Morning Coffee with Dan*, is heard throughout the Valley six days a week, Monday-Saturday, from 6-10am. On Fridays, the program is broadcast from the Hyatt Grand Champions Resort in Indian Wells with public service and celebrity guests such as Donald Trump, who said, "If you're not listening to Dan McGrath, you're fired!"

Much sought after as host, MC, guest speaker, interviewer, voice-over guy and DJ, Dan generously lends his support to many charities such as the American Cancer Society, the Special Olympics, the Desert Symphony, Desert AIDS Project, Barbara Sinatra Children's Center, golf tournaments and more. "I can't contribute millions of dollars, but I can give of my time and talent," he offers. For instance, he just hosted and participated in the inaugural golf tournament for The Childhelp Cheryl Ladd & John O'Hurley Golf Classic at Desert Willow Golf Resort.

For fun Dan plays golf, watches sports and works in his yard. "I love every day," he says. "I look forward to some other challenge that I know will come along. I'm a grateful, thankful kind of person and can't think of a better honor than my star."

Dan McGrath is to Palm Springs radio what his hero Johnny Carson was to late night talk shows…the best!

Whitey Mitchell ready for an important gig.

THIS ONE'S PERSONAL
GORDON "WHITEY" MITCHELL

STAR #266
DEDICATED FEBRUARY 20, 2006
128 S. PALM CANYON DR.

Gordon "Whitey" Mitchell loved life and lived it full of humor and appreciation for all he had been given. Born into a musical family, he took up the string bass in school and became a professional musician by age fifteen. He was nicknamed "Whitey" by fellow musicians. He studied radio and television at Syracuse University and then plunged into the New York jazz scene, becoming a regular at the famed nightspots Birdland and Basin Street East. He led his own groups at The Village Vanguard and The Embers and later toured with big band greats Benny Goodman and Pete Rugolo, played Carnegie Hall with Gene Krupa and appeared with Buddy Rich, Ella Fitzgerald, Dizzy Gillespie and Lester Young on tour with the famed concert series *Jazz at the Philharmonic*.

He worked with top artists Andre Previn, Charlie Ventura, Peggy Lee, Mel Torme, Billy Eckstine, Julie London, Jack Jones, and Frankie Randall, recorded with Anita O'Day, Barbra Streisand, and Anthony Newley, and played the bass solo introduction on Ben E. King's mega-hit record "Stand By Me." Whitey became a first-call studio musician, performing on hundreds of recording sessions, television and film scores and often placed in the *Metronome* and *Downbeat* jazz polls. He made six recordings with his own band and is listed in six music books, two of which are *Laughter from the Hip* and *The Biographical Encyclopedia of Jazz*.

In the early '60s, Whitey wrote a satirical piece for *Downbeat* magazine about a much-unloved society bandleader which attracted several letters to the editor, including one from the avant-garde comedian Lenny Bruce, who raved about his writing ability. With the additional encouragement

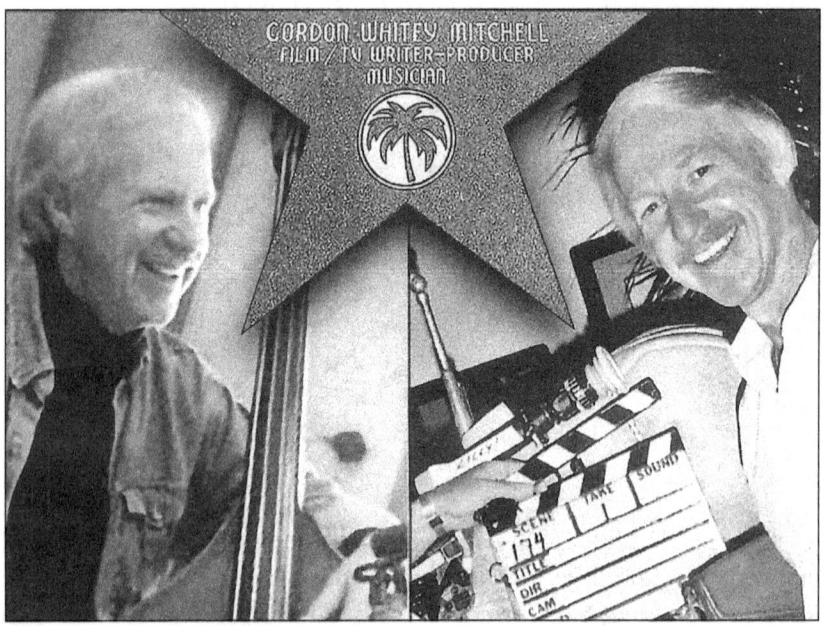

Whitey's two show-business careers.

of noted pianist/composer Andre Previn, Whitey moved to Los Angeles in 1965 to pursue a career in screenwriting and received his first script assignment in just five months. Whitey began a sabbatical from music to write and produce full time for such hit television shows as *All in the Family, Get Smart* (WGA nomination), *The Jeffersons* (Image Award nomination), *Good Times, Maude, Mork & Mindy, The Mary Tyler Moore Show, The Odd Couple, The Bob Hope Show, The Twilight Zone* and hundreds more, as well as many pilots. He wrote the feature film *Private Resort* starring Johnny Depp.

By 1995 the phone stopped ringing since anyone in Hollywood over the age of forty was deemed too old. An avid, low handicap golfer, Whitey suggested we move to the desert and reinvent ourselves. I agreed, since I had enough of television production and being an agent to writers who were no longer considered relevant.

Now a big fish in a little pond, Whitey was immediately offered, and I produced, a radio talk show, *The Power Lunch*, in which he interviewed celebrity guests from the entertainment world, followed by another show called *The Natural Golf Hour*. He simultaneously rekindled his love of the bass, playing in all the local entertainment venues, and recorded a CD, *Just In Time*.

Celebrating Whitey on star day. Left to right: Allan Blye-Producer, Elvis Presley and Sonny & Cher Shows; Marilyn; Whitey; Mort Lachman-Producer, Bob Hope Shows; Bill Asher-Director, I Love Lucy & Producer, Bewitched.

Next came a return to writing with a column for *Golf News*, an award-winning magazine then one for *Desert Entertainer Magazine*. For several years he taught classes on screenwriting, wrote plays and pilots, and was asked to join the board of directors of the Palm Springs Walk of Stars. It wasn't long before Whitey was awarded his own star in tribute to his two amazing careers, which sits in front of the Plaza Theatre. He's been inducted into his high school's Distinguished Alumni Hall of Fame. Whitey has written two books, which I edited: *Star Walk: A Guide to the Palm Springs Walk of Stars* and his autobiography *Hackensack To Hollywood:*

My Two Show Business Careers, which coincidentally can be ordered from *bearmanormedia.com*.

Whitey and I met in Hollywood on a television show called *The Good Life*. We married in six weeks. The show lasted only thirteen weeks, but our good life together lasted thirty-eight years. We lived in Camelot.

I no longer get calls after his round of golf asking what to bring home

for lunch. There is no more disagreement about how full the dishwasher should be before starting it, and the television is never on too loud. I no longer clean the greasy stove after his homemade bacon and egg Sunday breakfast. I have become the grandfather clock-winder now, but I don't hear his words of amazement at its accuracy, as he compared it to the atomic clock. And no one clicks off a certain conservative television station yelling, "F.U. Fox News!"

Throughout the 2008-09 election campaign Whitey was on the same page with Barack Obama and hoped to live until January 20 to see his inauguration. Although he didn't make it by three days, he did share the front page of our local newspaper with President Obama as the news of Whitey's passing was printed!

The love we shared was a gift. The alternative to my grief would be living in this world without ever having known him and the huge influence he had on my life. The pain I live with represents the love that was, and is, the richest portion of my life. Even in his physical absence, our relationship goes on. His inspiration and presence is a part of me. He still echoes within my thoughts and words and who he was and what he did has been woven into who I am.

Our last cruise. Whitey was a Guest Lecturer on comedy writing.

Gordon 'Whitey' Mitchell
February 22, 1932 - January 17, 2009
My Husband, My Best Friend, The Love of My Life

Grace and Phil Moody at work.

FIXTURES ON THE ENTERTAINMENT SCENE
GRACE & PHIL MOODY

STAR #29
DEDICATED APRIL 2, 1994
123 N. PALM CANYON DR.

Phil and the late Grace Moody have made an indelible mark on the entertainment scene for years.

Phil grew up in Southampton, England, and his dad, an officer in the British Navy and Chief Gunner on navy ships, warned Phil against getting into his line of work. "Okay, I'll take up music," he said and began piano lessons at an early age, which eventually led him to Britain's prestigious Royal Academy of Music where he graduated with honors. Phil and his musician brothers found gigs even during the horrors of World War II. They would trade jobs for food, walking to work during the Nazi bombing attacks, dodging bombs and an occasional air raid!

Phil accompanied many of England's top entertainers and worked with American singers as well, including the popular vocal group The Andrews Sisters. He later worked for the BBC writing and conducting radio shows, movies and television. When the war ended, Phil took everyone's advice and moved to Hollywood and was hired to compose music for the 1969 20th-Century Fox documentary *Footprints on the Moon*, which chronicles the events of the Apollo 11 moon landing. This opened the door to Universal-International and Warner Bros. who hired Moody to score music for films such as *So This Is Paris*, *The Second Greatest Sex* and *Love Me Deadly* . But enough about Phil.

Grace Moody made her stage debut, along with her sister, Pony, at the age of eleven. The Sherrell Sisters, as they were known, sang and danced their way through vaudeville. They performed on the radio show *Uncle Don's*, the most popular children's program of the time. Grace's mom, a stage mother, brought her girls to Hollywood to pursue their movie careers. While searching for an accompanist, Grace and Phil met and hit it off personally as well as musically, which pretty much put an end to the Sherrell Sisters as an act. No word on Mom's reaction.

Once married, the Moodys settled in the Los Angeles suburb of Sherman Oaks, as Phil continued his studio work, and in the '70s they relocated to Las Vegas where Phil wrote music and performed with Jimmy Durante, Mae West and the Ritz Brothers, among others. Somewhere along the way, daughter Mary showed up and in her teenage years they moved to Palm Springs to open and entertain in Moody's Supper Club. The club reigned for twelve years and became the "in" spot for tourists and the movie crowd. When Moody's closed, they brought their act to Liveri's Celebrity Room; the act now included daughter Mary (who is married to a wonderful drummer, Jay Lewis). The Moodys performed a cabaret-style revue called *A Swinging Salute to Sinatra* and ended each show with a song written by Phil and another prolific songwriter, the late Buddy Kaye, called "My Town is Palm Springs." The tune was recorded on a CD by immensely talented local singer Mike Costley and is one of the songs used by the Walk of Stars at the dedications.

While Grace is sorely missed, we still have Phil Moody and we're glad he successfully managed to avoid all of Hitler's bombs!

The New Christy Minstrels. Randy Sparks on left, front row.

ON THE ROAD AGAIN
THE NEW CHRISTY MINSTRELS AND RANDY SPARKS

STAR #318
DEDICATED JANUARY 12, 2009
538 NO. PALM CANYON DR.

It's hard to keep up with this extraordinary group who play to mostly sold-out audiences from Maine to Arizona and Washington State to North Carolina, performing thirty-three shows in fifty-four days! This year The New Christy Minstrels are celebrating fifty years of bringing American folk music to the world!

Founder, singer/guitarist Randy Sparks was born into a church-going musical family and has been writing songs since early childhood. Once he heard his idol, actor, writer and folk singer Burl Ives on the radio, he knew what he wanted to do when he grew up, and for many years he toured with his mentor and friend as his opening act and songwriter.

Sparks started with his own trio in 1961, which later merged with another trio and added additional musicians to create a vocal ensemble. It didn't take long for the ten-piece group to record their first album, *Presenting the New Christy Minstrels*, which garnered a Grammy Award for Best Performance by a Chorus. They moved on to success as regulars on *The Andy Williams Show*, frequently played at L.A.'s legendary Troubadour nightspot, performed at Carnegie Hall, The Copacabana and in President Johnson's White House.

Randy tells this story from his early days on the road: He was working solo and as he finished his show, a man approached to advise he'd be better off going back where he came from, that he didn't have what it takes. Eight years later, that same man presented Sparks with his Grammy Award. He was singer and actor Gordon MacRae.

"I invented the concept and wrote most of the songs the group sings," he says. "I've always had the preconceived notion that everyone should be a perfect singer, like a choir in harmony, on and off the stage." A few of the famous alumnae whose careers Randy helped launch are Kenny Rogers (who left to form The First Edition), Gene Clark (The Byrds), and Larry Ramos (The Association). Although not an alumnae, Randy can take credit for discovering, writing for and naming John Denver, aka John Deutschendordf.

"This is the best team I've ever put together," he continued. "It's a matter of chemistry. Each one is a gifted solo artist and everyone is an exemplary human being." Randy's dream team of today brings their unique blend of humor and music to the stage.

Among the New Christy Minstrel's hundreds of recordings on more than thirty albums are the hits "Green, Green," "Far Side of the Hill," "Puff the Magic Dragon," "We'll Sing in the Sunshine," and "This Land Is Your Land." Most of these songs were written by Sparks and were *Billboard* chart-toppers.

I asked him to describe what it's really like to be constantly on the road now that they're in their 60s and 70s: "It's far better than years ago. We older folks feast on the scenery, the people and the geography. We were treated like cattle in olden times, overworked and cheated. Now we work for the people in the seats and for ourselves and our Foundation. Our concerts are the most fun an older person can have… for us and for the audience, and we've never done a show without a standing ovation."

A cancer survivor, Randy's doctor has prescribed a stress-free environment and he says he's found it.

Randy and the group have established the New Christy Minstrels Foundation. "Painless History" is a free-of-charge teaching program, hidden in the form of entertainment, wherein students learn about American history. They create songs about historical facts, such as telling the kids in song that Lewis & Clark were just on the world's most ambitious camping trip. "How else can you get kids to care?" he asks.

For more on Randy Sparks and The New Christy Minstrels, go to *thenewchristyminstrels.com*.

Frankie Randall.

SINATRA'S PAL
FRANKIE RANDALL

STAR #209
DEDICATED MAY 12, 2001
155 S. PALM CANYON DR.

The most famous former resident of Clifton, New Jersey, and son of a professional musician, Frankie Randall decided on his career one special night when he and his father caught a performance of his piano player cousin bowing to thunderous applause while playing with a big band. He said, "Dad, that's what I want to do!" So at seven years old, Dad bought his son a piano, gave him lessons and Frankie played his first gig at age thirteen!

The most popular kid in his high-school class, he was known as "Chico" Randall, derived from his Italian name, Francisco. While attending college, he hired a booking agent, got work in the Catskills and throughout New York, and met famed restaurateur Jilly Rizzo, who was so impressed with Frankie he offered him a job in his hot-spot club, Jilly's. Frankie remembers one night: "I looked up from the piano and there he was… Frank Sinatra! I couldn't believe it!" After closing, Sinatra asked Frankie to join his table, and a lifelong friendship began.

Sinatra recommended Frankie to the vice president of RCA Records who offered him a recording session which led to several albums and dozens of CD's. Then Sinatra suggested Frankie to Jack Entratta, of the Sands Hotel in Las Vegas, and Frankie opened for Joey Bishop.

It seems everyone noticed Frankie Randall's immense talent. The hotel magnate Steve Wynn hired him to play the Golden Nugget in Atlantic

City and, after six months, made him entertainment coordinator for the lounge. Before long, Wynn moved Frankie to the main showroom, where he booked his pal, Frank Sinatra, as well as Dean Martin, Sammy Davis and Liza Minnelli. Fast forward several years and after hundreds of recordings, performances, bookings and even acting, Frankie moved to Rancho Mirage, California, to retire. But the retirement was a failure. Apparently, the only thing Frankie isn't good at is kicking back and doing nothing.

When Ol' Blue Eyes announced his own retirement, Frankie asked if he could have some of his arrangements. Sinatra's reply: "You can have anything you want. It's great to have a guy like you who'll continue my music after I'm gone." The next thing Frankie knew, "A FedEx truck pulls up to the house with all these arrangements by Nelson Riddle, Billy May, Neil Hefti and Quincy Jones!" And just like his mentor, Frankie works with the best arrangers and musicians. For example, Frankie and my late husband, screenwriter-musician Whitey Mitchell, who was his bass player back in New Jersey, wrote and recorded a song together. It's called "Marilyn" and was performed as a surprise on our 25th wedding anniversary party.

Frankie performed a Frank Sinatra tribute show at Casino Morongo in Banning, California, and then did a stint as entertainment director. He conceived and starred in a musical extravaganza, *Sinatra, My Way*, with the Pat Rizzo twenty-piece band and six dancers. They completed 150 successful performances at the Annenberg Theatre in Palm Springs.

Frankie has produced and performed his original concept, *That's Italian*, at the McCallum Theatre in Palm Desert and other venues. He's presented another original show, *Last Call at Jilly's*, which features Frankie, his band and famous celebrity guests, as they recall the swinging days at Jilly's.

"Life is wonderful now," Frankie says. "I choose where and when to work and only take what appeals to me. Besides, it's great not to work New Year's Eve!" For more on Frankie Randall or to purchase his CD's, go to *frankierandall.com*.

Melinda Read arrives for her star ceremony in a hansom carriage.

THE TALK OF THE TOWN
MELINDA READ

STAR #254
DEDICATED APRIL 30, 2005
144 S. PALM CANYON DR.

Melinda Read started life in Lynnwood, Washington, a suburb of Seattle. A veteran radio personality by age six, she would sit on the station manager's lap, who happened to be her dad, and read the commercials and station IDs.

In her teenage years, Melinda entered modeling school, participated in fashion shows and became Miss Teenage America in a competition which aired on ABC's *Wide World of Entertainment*. She toured the state of Washington, made speaking engagements on national television and returned home to compete again in several additional beauty pageants over the years. Following high school, Melinda enrolled in a college of art and design, The Fashion Institute of Technology, in New York City, returning home again after graduation to earn a BA at Seattle Pacific University. During this time, Melinda got busy buying and developing up to fifteen radio stations. "I did everything," she says, "from scrubbing toilets and painting walls to hiring and broadcasting...whatever had to be done to make the stations profitable." Yet, she still found time to enter beauty pageants and won Mrs. Washington America!

Coming to the desert since the late '70s, Melinda purchased a home in La Quinta in the mid-'90s and competed in and won Mrs. California International, which led her into television. Time-Warner noticed Melinda and moved her into public affairs programming, where she hosted a half-hour program that later developed into her own premier celebrity guest interview show, *Talk of the Desert,* seen anytime on Time-Warner On Demand. She has hosted and produced this show for thirteen years and recently completed her 500th episode! Melinda has interviewed such notables as Jack Jones, Carol Channing, Rich Little, Barbara Sinatra, Frankie Randall, Shirley Jones and countless others.

Afflicted with type 1 diabetes since age three, Melinda is the poster girl for the Desert Diabetes Club and her tireless support has no doubt boosted their efforts to raise money and find a cure.

For many years Melinda has hosted and emceed for the annual "Jim Cook Day of Hope for Diabetes," a free event which is held every year at Eisenhower Medical Center in Rancho Mirage, California. Experts speak on the latest research relating to diabetes and their educational talks highlight weight management, exercise, medications and other essentials to controlling this dreaded disease. "Knowledge is power," says Melinda. "A Day of Hope provides important information about diabetes." For more information, go to *www.emc.org/ddc.*

You can tell this is one busy lady…overseeing radio stations, hosting a TV show and speaking for diabetes. As an actress, she appeared in an episode of *Will & Grace*, hosted a real estate show in Las Vegas called *Builder's Showcase* and is assistant producer for the musical productions *That's Italian* and *Last Call at Jilly's.*

"Success," Melinda says, "means the realization of what I already have. I'm living my dream…to be on television. Life is wonderful."

Debbie Reynolds.

SHE'S STAYING UNTIL SHE'S THE ONLY ONE LEFT!
DEBBIE REYNOLDS

STAR #174
DEDICATED JANUARY 4, 2000
155 S. PALM CANYON DR.

Mary Frances Reynolds made her stage debut winning a high-school talent contest and caught the eye of a couple of studio talent scouts. Following a screen test, she was signed as a contract player by Jack Warner who gave her the name Debbie. Although she says she stumbled into show business, once she started singing, dancing and acting, she never looked back. And taking her cues from the late centenarian, comedian George Burns she says, "I'm going to stay in show business until I'm the only one left!"

After a couple Warner Bros. films, MGM stole Debbie away and signed her to a seven-year contract. She was cast with Gene Kelly and Donald O'Connor in the all-time classic musical *Singin' in the Rain*. "I was learning how to dance on the set and on one particularly discouraging day, I crawled under the piano, crying." she recalls. "Fred Astaire happened to be visiting. He peeked under the piano, offered me his hand and said, 'Come out of there and follow me.' He told me to follow his steps and after about an hour, he said, 'Now, don't forget, if you're not sweating, you're not learning.'"

Reynolds learned her lesson well. She went on to appear with Fred Astaire and Red Skelton in *Three Little Words*, winning a Golden Globe nomination, and then as Jane Powell's sister in *Two Weeks With Love*, followed by *Susan Slept Here*, *The Tender Trap*, *Bundle Of Joy* (with then-husband Eddie Fisher), *Tammy and the Bachelor*, *The Unsinkable Molly Brown* (for which she received an Oscar nomination), earned a Gold Record for her recording of "Tammy," and won an Emmy nomination for her portrayal as Grace's mother on TV's *Will & Grace*. I stopped counting her feature film and television credits at eighty and awards at forty-five.

Today, Reynolds' primary career focus is on her nightclub act. She remains a popular headliner in the casino circuit. Already booked in six states across the nation this year, I asked how long she plans to keep up this demanding pace: "It's the people," she says. "Travelling around is hard, entertaining is not. When I get out there on that stage and share myself with the audience, I know it's all worthwhile."

Always one to want to give something back, Debbie started The Thailians in 1957, a group of industry professionals who donate their time and talent to raise money for mentally disturbed children and other causes. As president Debbie has tirelessly helped raise more than $30 million over the years. Their main fundraising event is the annual Thailians gala, which last year honored Hugh Hefner at the Playboy mansion.

Over thirty years ago, Debbie opened the Debbie Reynolds Dance Studio in North Hollywood, and shows up every chance she gets. It's attracted the likes of Michael Jackson, Bette Midler, Cher and others. "Whenever, and if, I do retire, I'll go back to teaching there," she says.

Debbie's dream was always to create the Hollywood Motion Picture Museum to showcase her vast collection of movie memorabilia from the major studios and the Harold Lloyd and Mary Pickford Estates, among others. Included in the 5,000-article collection, which was auctioned off last June in Los Angeles, was Marilyn Monroe's subway dress from *The Seven Year Itch*, (which sold for a cool 4.5 million), Barbra Streisand's *Hello, Dolly!* dress, Judy Garland's *Wizard of Oz* blue dress, costumes worn by Audrey Hepburn, Gene Kelly, Bette Davis, Marlon Brando, Harpo Marx and others. The collection garnered a record-breaking 22.8 million in sales.

Debbie Reynolds owns what may be a record three stars on the Hollywood Walk of Fame, foot and hand prints at Grauman's Chinese Theatre and a star on the Walk of Stars. When not on tour, her passion is her family, friends and collecting. She remains close to daughter, actress-writer Carrie Fisher, and son, commercial TV director Todd Fisher, who once commented, "Some people, if they're looking for their mother, would go to the kitchen. I'd go to Vegas!"

Del Shores.

TEXAS CHARMER
DEL SHORES

STAR #276
DEDICATED OCTOBER 5, 2006
538 N. PALM CANYON DR.

Many gifted entertainment industry icons were born in unlikely places and Del Shores, who grew up in the tiny town of Winters, Texas, is no exception. "I was raised with talent all around me," he says. "My father was a Southern Baptist preacher and a speaker. Mother was a high-school drama teacher and a director. My aunt was a country singer who recorded albums with her own band."

Bitten by the acting bug early, Del's mom always said, "No, no. You don't do that for a living!" But in time she supported her son's decision and enjoyed his success when she and Dad attended the premiere of *Sordid Lives* in Dallas. "I was worried about the profanity, but they did okay with it," he says.

Del launched his career in 1987 with his play, the black comedy *Daddy's Dyin' Who's Got The Will?*, which ran for two years in Hollywood. He penned the movie version three years later, which starred Beau Bridges and Tess Harper.

Best known for his hilarious, campy film *Sordid Lives*, it became a cult favorite and deals with a dysfunctional family coming together for a relative's funeral. The film, made for a mere half-million dollars, stars Olivia Newton-John, Beau Bridges and others. I asked how much of his own life is reflected in the film: "The core of *Sordid Lives* is taken from my own experiences…with embellishments," he points out. "Aunt Sissy is modeled after one aunt, LaVonda, after Aunt Rita and Latrelle, after my mother." With a devoted fan base in Palm Springs, *Sordid Lives* was the longest-running film in its history. "It ran for ninety-six weeks," says Shores. "It was the most amazing moment when we first arrived at the Camelot Theater for the one-year anniversary of its run. We had no idea it had become such a huge hit. It was a 'wow' moment for me."

Sordid Lives the TV series made its debut in 2008. Shores wrote, produced and directed the show's twelve episodes that aired on MTV's gay-themed LOGO cable channel, geared toward the LGBT community. The series starred Rue McClanahan and Olivia Newton-John.

I asked Del which one of his many works is his favorite: "Closest to my heart is *Southern Baptist Sissies*. This was my journey into learning to accept myself as a gay man. It took me a couple of years to write." Like several of his other plays, *Sissies* enjoyed a long run at the 99-seat equity waiver Zephyr Theater in Los Angeles. Happy in his new life as a performer, as well as writer-director, these days Del tours with his intimate one-man show, *Del Shores: Sordid Confessions*, in which he shares his personal experiences that have inspired all those plays and movies.

Del has completed the screenplay of perhaps his most critically acclaimed play, *The Trials and Tribulations of a Trailer Trash Housewife*, now in pre-production.

Although he's at home on both sides of the camera, I asked Del which hat he's most comfortable wearing: "I'm a storyteller first, so it's writing. But, then, what I love to do is direct what I've written." And who would he most like to work with? "Meryl Streep," he answered decisively. "We pay tribute to her in *Yellow*. I won't work with anyone who has a bad reputation."

Del estimates he's received maybe a hundred awards, if those for actors are included. "I don't know exactly how many, but I'm running out of space." To name a few awards: L.A. Weekly Theater, Drama-Logue, L.A. Drama Critics Circle, GLAAD Media, NAACP Theater, Back Stage West Garland and the New York Int'l Independent Film & Video Festival.

His favorite line from *Southern Baptist Sissies* is "Sometimes I close my eyes and create a perfect world," to which he adds, "I hope for a better world." We hope for more of Del Shores!

Shores is currently performing again, touring the country in his sold-out one-man show, Del Shores Sordid Confessions.

Barbara Sinatra.

SHE DOES IT HER WAY!

BARBARA SINATRA

STAR #119
DEDICATED FEBRUARY 4, 1998
123 NO. PALM CANYON DR.

We like longtime desert resident Barbara Sinatra and the feeling is mutual. You are probably aware of her brainchild, the Barbara Sinatra Children's Center.

Barbara Blakely was born in Missouri and raised in Kansas. She became a Las Vegas showgirl, a model and a charm school instructor. Fast forward to the mid-'70s when she met and married Frank Sinatra and for twenty-five years the two of them brightened the Southern California social and charity scene immeasurably.

As Barbara became more involved with charity work, a doctor friend asked her to help with a program for sexually abused children. "Once I met the children, I was hooked," she says. They started raising funds with profitable celebrity art auctions and formed a board of directors. They soon realized they needed a venue and Barbara called her good friend, the late publisher and philanthropist Walter Annenberg to ask for help. Once he understood how committed Barbara was to the project, he generously arranged for the land, the architect and the builder, and in 1986 the Barbara Sinatra Children's Center was founded at the Eisenhower Medical Center campus in Rancho Mirage, California. "Our mission," Barbara says, "is to counsel abused children, give them the tools they need for a productive, happy life and to break the cycle of generational abuse."

Mr. & Mrs. Sinatra pledged that no child would be turned away because of their inability to pay, which meant they would need ongoing funding. And so, a golf tournament was born. Frank easily persuaded his buddies Sammy and Dean and that crowd to sign up, and he called it "his little party in the desert."

Now known as the Frank Sinatra Starkey Hearing Foundation Charity

Invitational Golf Tournament, held each year in February, its sponsors are Fantasy Springs Resort Casino, the Eagle Falls Golf Course, Jack Daniels (Sinatra's favorite) and Starkey. The popular two-day celebrity-amateur event offers dinner parties, entertainment, auctions and a luncheon fashion show, all dedicated to Frank Sinatra's music and memory.

Participating celebrity golfers have been Pat Boone, Tom Dreesen, Frankie Randall, Patrick Evans, Peter Marshall, Michael Dante, Elke Sommer, Fred Williamson and many others.

A complimentary open house at the Children's Center is held the next day, which includes a continental breakfast. "I always want the town to come and take a tour," Barbara says. "It's so gratifying to see how what we're doing here changes the lives of the children and parents."

Sinatra has also been involved with Childhelp USA and the Princess Grace Foundation. Several deserving awards have been conferred on her, including Woman of the Year from the women's recovery program Friendly House and the Palm Springs Women in Film & Television's Jackie Lee Houston Humanitarian Award. The Angel View group recognized her with their Angel of the Year Award.

Her new book, *Lady Blue Eyes: My Life with Frank*, has recently been released and can be ordered at Amazon.com and other sites.

Barbara Sinatra's star, just as in their life together, sits right next to her husband's on the Palm Springs Walk of Stars.

Ol' Blue Eyes.

CLOSE ENCOUNTERS OF THE CELEBRITY KIND
FRANK SINATRA

STAR #18
DEDICATED JANUARY 15, 1994
123 N. PALM CANYON DR.

Most likely there is nothing about this larger-than-life, giant of a man you don't already know. He's probably touched the lives of everyone in this book. So you've already been reading about him subliminally. That's why I'm simply going to tell of my own personal encounter.

My dear, late screenwriter/musician (bassist) husband, Gordon "Whitey" Mitchell, regularly worked with friend and fellow star recipient, singer/pianist/composer Frankie Randall. Their gig on this particular evening was a cocktail party held in an opulent private residence in the exclusive Thunderbird Estates section of Rancho Mirage. The party was part of the Frank Sinatra Celebrity Invitational Golf Tournament; the last one Sinatra would attend before he became too ill. I was lucky enough to also be invited.

"Oh, my God!" I said to Whitey. "I could be sitting on a couch with Frank Sinatra. What am I going to wear? What am I going to do? What am I going to say?!"

We arrived early so Whitey could set up his bass and amplifier and be ready to play as soon as the first guests arrived. As I stood there in the living room waiting for the party to begin, through my peripheral vision I became aware of something orange approaching me. (Orange was Sinatra's favorite color.) "Hello," he said, "can I get you a drink?" Although stunned, I managed to answer, "Yes!" And then, silence. I thought, he's going to wait on me? "So, what would you like?" he requested. "Oh…I'll have orange juice," I blurted out, no more wanting orange juice than a glass of milk. He crossed to the bar, came back with the dreaded juice and his own drink (Jack Daniels), and lifted his glass to our mutual "Cheers!" We clinked and sat down on the couch!

Later, a chosen few of us were invited to stay for dinner and Sinatra's place was to my right at the head of the table. His wife, Barbara, was seated at the other end. I could have Frank all to myself and couldn't believe my luck. With my new-found self-assurance, I was looking forward to more conversation with my new best friend, except he didn't feel well and his chair next to me sat empty. I missed him.

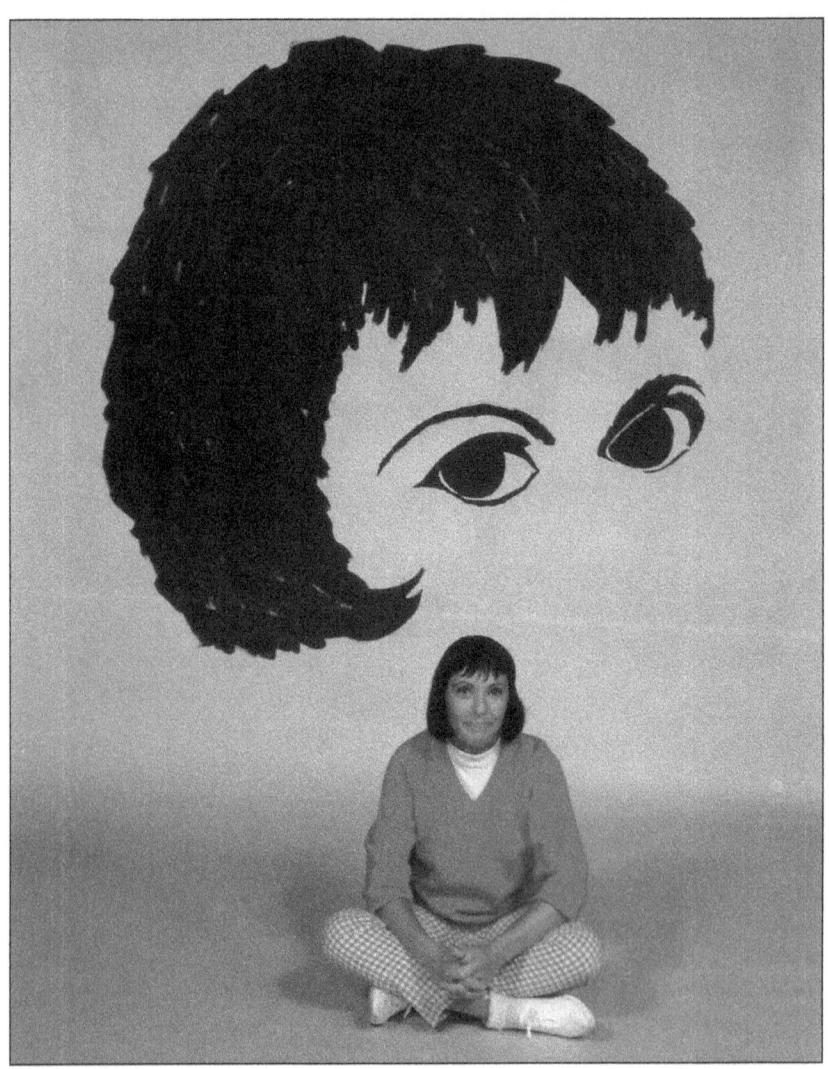

Keely Smith.

SHE WISHES US LOVE
KEELY SMITH

STAR #129
DEDICATED OCTOBER 13, 1998
121 SO. PALM CANYON DR.

Dorothy Keely, who became Keely Smith, grew up with the gift of song. Encouraged by her aunt while still a pre-teen, she auditioned for *Joe Brown's Radio Gang* and became a regular on that popular Saturday morning kids' radio show in her hometown of Norfolk, Virginia. Keely went on to sing with a naval air station band and by age sixteen, was a paid professional, singing with the Earl Bennett Band at a time when America was crazy about dance, swing and big band music.

Her career really got going, she says, "When I saw Louie Prima, the love of my life, at the Steel Pier in Atlantic City, and auditioned for him." She sang only two songs before he hired her on the spot! They became an item, married in 1953, and got busy touring and recording for Capitol Records during the '50s and later for Dot Records. Among their many successful albums was the Top 20 hit "That Old Black Magic," which won them the first-ever Grammy Award in 1958. On her show, Dinah Shore introduced them as "The greatest nightclub act in the country." Keely recorded on her own as well with such legendary composers/arrangers as Nelson Riddle and Billy May. Her first solo album, her favorite, *I Wish You Love*, sold over a million copies and went gold.

Throughout the '50s, Louie and Keely's nightclub act, featuring Sam Butera and the Witnesses, was a mainstay of the Las Vegas entertainment scene. Her dead-pan and seemingly uninterested on-stage attitude was a hit with fans, a routine that was "borrowed" by Sonny and Cher years later. Performing five shows a night at the Sahara Hotel, from midnight to 6:00am, they consistently packed the house, and among the regulars were none other than Frank Sinatra, Natalie Wood & Robert Wagner, Howard Hughes, Sammy Davis, Jr. and Senator John F. Kennedy.

Louie and Keely raised two beautiful daughters, Toni Elizabeth and Luanne Prima, and after parting Keely put her career on hold for a time to raise them. With her own singing group, The Jive Aces, Toni sometimes opens for Mom. Toni is producing a work-in-progress musical show, entitled *The Wildest*, and says: "Growing up with two such mega-talents as my parents was just normal and natural to me. I'm grateful it afforded me lovely opportunities to pursue my acting ambition." Keely remains close to her daughters, as well as her son-in-law, pianist-composer-arranger Dennis Michaels, who happens to be her musical director and accompanist and who also happens to be married to daughter Toni. Keely's brother, "Piggy," formerly served as her road manager. Nepotism, you say? That's okay, as long as they keep it in the family!

Keely has made hundreds of recordings and also appeared in several movies and videos. Among her many albums and CD's are *Swing, Swing, Swing, Keely Swings Basie Style, with Strings, Vegas '58-Today* and the Grammy nominated *Keely Sings Sinatra*. She performed at President John F. Kennedy's inauguration and has been doubly honored, one star in Palm Springs and one on the Hollywood Walk of Fame.

Keely continues to tour worldwide, playing to delighted, sell-out crowds. She performed at the annual New Orleans Jazz & Heritage Festival as Louie Prima was honored on his 100th birthday year and she's booked at the Cerritos Center for Performing Arts for Valentine's Day.

When I asked if there's anything career-wise she has missed, her reply was a clear-cut, "Yes! I would like to do a Broadway play!"

Susan Stafford.

STOP THE WHEEL, SHE WANTS TO GET OFF!

SUSAN STAFFORD

STAR #258
DEDICATED OCTOBER 15, 2005
193 S. PALM CANYON DR.

Susan Stafford made her stage debut as a teenager when she won a beauty contest and then began a modeling career. She came to Hollywood to pursue an acting career in movies and television, which included guest-starring on such hit television shows as *Marcus Welby, MD, Love, American Style, Police Story* and *Hawaii Five-O*. In addition, Susan hosted her own syndicated radio show and was a newspaper columnist for the *Los Angeles Times*. But Susan may be best known as the original hostess on the game show *Wheel of Fortune* and is the first woman to get a microphone, to make her own clothing deal and the first woman ever nominated for an Emmy on a game show.

Susan was briefly married to Dick Ebersol of NBC Sports and just after they exchanged vows on a Malibu beach, Chevy Chase threw her in the ocean. Later, Susan served as vice president for Barry & Enright Productions and for seven years partnered, until his passing, with game show creator/producer Dan Enright. Using her production experience, Susan worked with Surgeon General C. Everett Koop on documentaries for America's leprosy missions in India, Africa and the Philippines. For her many charitable efforts, Susan is one of the recipients of the World Unity Award for Humanitarian Service. Among Susan's many other accomplishments, is a Master Degree and a Ph.D. in Clinical Psychology.

Stafford is happy to have her star sandwiched between her close friends Rock Hudson (she was with him in his last days) and George Nader. In fact, the Rock Hudson Estate sponsored her star as well as the three celebration parties that followed…one at the former Tony Martin & Cyd Charisse home, one at the Rock Hudson estate and one at Mel Haber's legendary Ingleside Inn. Of her star day, Susan says, "I felt so loved by my family and friends. The memory will live in my heart forever."

Susan has several projects in the works, including a movie, a television game/reality show and the franchise for the Miss Teenage America contests. She recently published her autobiography, *Stop the Wheel, I Want to Get Off*, which is available on her website Susan Stafford.com.

The Walk of Stars board was so captivated with Susan they asked her not only to join them as one of their directors, but to serve as their money maven, the treasurer.

Connie Stevens.

THE POSTER GIRL FOR MULTI-TASKING
CONNIE STEVENS

STAR #31
DEDICATED MAY 20, 1994
214 N. PALM CANYON DR.

The Walk of Stars has a number of honorees with a wide range of interests and talents, but Connie Stevens outshines them all. Film, television and Broadway star, singer, recording artist, nightclub performer, businesswoman, humanitarian, writer, director, producer, film editor and former Screen Actors Guild board member, she's the poster girl for multi-tasking.

Born to musician-performer parents, Concetta Rosalie Ann Ingolia took her dad's stage name of Stevens as her own. After moving from Brooklyn to LA, she sang with the vocal group The Letterman and the Three Debs in her teen years and attended a professional school, studying music and dance and found work in teen films. Jerry Lewis discovered her at Paramount and cast her in his film *Rock-A-Bye Baby*. "I was so naïve," she says, "I followed the crew's prank telling me to go to the bike shop to get chains so I wouldn't get a shock on the soundstage."

Warner Bros. bought Stevens' Paramount contract and cast her in the successful series *Hawaiian Eye* with Robert Conrad. "While filming one day," she recounts, "I get a phone call from Elvis Presley. I couldn't believe it. He invited me to a party. We dated for a year and remained lifelong friends."

Connie starred with George Burns in TV's *Wendy and Me*, as well as on Broadway in Neil Simon's *Star Spangled Girl* with Anthony Perkins. Among her other films are *Grease 2, Back to the Beach* and *Palm Springs*

Weekend, filmed guess where? She met her first husband, actor Jim Stacy, on that film. Some of her television work includes *Maverick, 77 Sunset Strip, Baywatch* and *The Love Boat*. Warner Bros. Records signed her as their first artist and she came up with three hits: a duet with Edd "Kookie" Burns, "Kookie Kookie, Lend Me Your Comb," "Too Young To Go Steady" and the early '60s #1 hit, "Sixteen Candles."

Stevens made numerous trips overseas doing USO Christmas Specials and says those are her most treasured moments on any stage. "My fondest memories are landing in Da Nang and performing on stage with Bob Hope for 40,000 shouting soldiers." For her work with our veterans, Connie was presented with the Bob Hope Award of Excellence at a gala at the Ronald Reagan Library.

Among her additional humanitarian ventures is a project she founded called Windfeather, which provides scholarships for Native-American Indian kids and funding for summer camp. She's also received recognition awards from the Shriner's Hospital, the Sons of Italy and the U.S. Armed Forces.

Comfortable on both sides of the camera, Connie made her directorial debut with *A Healing*, a 1997 award-winning documentary about a group of Red Cross nurses who return to their workplace in Vietnam. She wrote, produced and directed a second film, *Saving Grace B. Jones*, based on her own experience as a young girl when she was witness to a murder. It stars Tatum O'Neal and Michael Biehn. Her latest project is a period piece, *Prairie Bones*.

A savvy businesswoman, Stevens created a cosmetic company called (symbolic of her persona) Forever Spring, producing popular, best-selling skin, makeup and fragrance products. For more information, go to Foreverspring.com.

Even as she continues to headline on the casino circuit and perform in concert, Connie still loves to spend quality time with her adored grandchildren and her two actress daughters from her marriage to the late Eddie Fisher.

I asked Connie when she realized she made it: "When my daughter and I went to Alaska. We stepped into an Eskimo hut in a remote village. We were covered in furry warm clothing. A man was carving ivory. He looked up at me and asked, 'Are you Connie Stevens?'"

Jerry Vale.

FRANK LOVED JERRY

JERRY VALE

STAR #138
DEDICATED DECEMBER 5, 1998
275 S. PALM CANYON DRIVE

Singing since childhood, Genaro Louis Vitaliano grew up in the Bronx and as a young lad took a shoeshine boy job in a barbershop where he sang while he worked. The boss liked his singing so much that he paid for his vocal lessons. Jerry sang in high-school musicals, won a talent contest and moved on to paying gigs around the city.

Pop singer Guy Mitchell arranged to have Jerry record demonstration records for Capitol Records, but they were more interested in Jerry's voice than the demo discs and signed him to a recording contract. He remained with Capitol throughout his entire career, recording a total of fifty albums, including such hits as "Have You Looked Into Your Heart," "Inamorata," "Pretend You Don't See Her," "Arrivederci, Roma" and his signature song, "Al Di La."

In 1952 Jerry met Frank Sinatra at Jack Dempsey's on Broadway and a lifelong friendship began. Sinatra brought Jerry to Las Vegas to do four weeks at the Sands Hotel, which turned into twenty-two weeks, four shows a night. Jerry tells a story when Sinatra bought his first plane, a DC-9, and wanted Jerry to see it, along with some other Vegas movers and shakers. Sinatra finished his last show at 2:00a.m., but Jerry didn't finish his show until 3:30a.m. So Sinatra and friends waited in Sinatra's dressing room until Jerry got there and the group set off to check out the plane. They were all amazed! They said, "Frank doesn't wait for anybody!"

"That's how much Frank loved Jerry," said Jerry's wife, Rita. And until Sinatra's death, Jerry and Rita spent Sundays at his Beverly Hills home, having dinner and playing cards. Vale remains involved with the Barbara Sinatra Children's Center and has been a regular at the Frank Sinatra tournament since it began.

Every year Jerry attends the NIAF Awards (National Italian American Foundation) in Washington, D.C., where he has performed. The event, which promotes the heritage and culture of Americans of Italian descent, has been attended by every sitting president. Another distinction Jerry received was the Ellis Island Medal of Honor from the National Ethnic Coalition.

A baseball fan since childhood (he would play on the streets of the Bronx), Jerry owned a triple "A" farm team called the Daytona Beach Admirals, which he sold to the New York Mets. He would sing the National Anthem at Yankee Stadium and Joe DiMaggio took Jerry's Gold Record to the Baseball Hall of Fame in Cooperstown, New York, where that Gold Record of "The Star Spangled Banner" still hangs.

These days, Jerry likes to watch his beloved baseball with his pals. The Vales celebrated their 53nd wedding anniversary and when I asked what plans they're making for the future, they said, "No plans. We just want to be healthy, enjoy the grandkids and maybe visit Jerry's star."

Think she was happy on star day?

FARM GIRL TO SEX SYMBOL
MAMIE VAN DOREN

STAR #261
DEDICATED DECEMBER 3, 2005
101 SO. PALM CANYON DR.

Former South Dakota farm girl Mamie Van Doren's first brush with fame was when, encouraged by her mom while still in her teens, she entered a beauty contest and won! As the newly crowned Miss Palm Springs, famed producer-aviator Howard Hughes, who was in the audience, discovered her. They became an item for a number of years while he launched her career, casting her in several RKO pictures. "He was so eccentric and private even then," she says. "He'd send a car for me at the Racquet Club…an old Chevy!"

Mamie made a few pictures for RKO in which she appeared with Robert Mitchum, Jane Russell and Vincent Price. She also posed for Alberto Vargas, the famous pin-up girl artist, whose painting of her appeared on the cover of *Esquire Magazine*. Studio executives at Universal-International noticed Mamie and, hoping for the next Marilyn Monroe who was under contract to 20th Century-Fox, signed Mamie to a seven-year contract. That's when Joan Oleander became Mamie Van Doren.

At Universal and other studios, Mamie made several pictures, including *Star in the Dust*, *Teacher's Pet* with Clark Gable and *High School Confidential!* She has made more than fifty films, many of them with Hollywood's greatest leading men of the time. On the stage, she performed in productions of *Gentlemen Prefer Blondes*, *Will Success Spoil Rock Hunter?* and *The Tender Trap*.

During the Vietnam War, Mamie entertained the troops in two three-month tours, including visiting hospital wards of amputees and burn victims, an unpopular stop with other celebrities. Even today she continues her charity efforts, working with AIDS victims.

Mamie was married for a time to big band leader Ray Anthony and sang with his band. She appeared on his television variety series, *The Ray Anthony Show*, and he appeared in a few of her movies. Nothing like a little nepotism, as long as it's in the family! A sports fan since childhood, she was engaged to baseball player star pitcher Bo Belinsky, dated baseball Hall of Famer Joe DiMaggio and football Hall of Famer Joe Namath. She enjoys a close friendship with Los Angeles Lakers' owner Jerry Buss, who invested in one of her movies, and has a standing invitation to sit in Buss' VIP suite at the Staples Center.

In her tell-all autobiography, *Playing the Field*, she reveals relationships with many Hollywood men and describes life as a media sex symbol. She was known as one of the "Three M's"…Marilyn Monroe, Jayne Mansfield and Mamie Van Doren. Although they were close friends, she's never been a Marilyn Monroe wannabe. She says she's always been comfortable in her own skin.

Mamie Van Doren has two stars. One she received from the Hollywood Walk of Fame in 1994 on the Boulevard near the legendary Grauman's Chinese Theatre and one in Palm Springs, which is positioned between Marlene Dietrich and her friend, Marilyn Monroe.

Dick Van Patten.

EIGHTY IS NOT ENOUGH
DICK VAN PATTEN

STAR #301
DEDICATED JANUARY 12, 2008
125 E. TAHQUITZ CANYON WAY

Dick Van Patten started life in Queens, New York, as the son of avid theatre-going parents. His mom was a stage mother to end all stage mothers who trekked him up and down Broadway to meet the decision makers until little Dickie won a part in *Tapestry In Gray* at age seven, and then moved on to appear in a dozen or so productions throughout his teenage years.

In 1946 Dick landed a part in *O Mistress Mine*, beating out several other hopefuls, most notably Marlon Brando. "It's still my most challenging and favorite role," he says. Van Patten played the son of then-major stars, the acclaimed husband-and-wife team Alfred Lunt and Lynn Fontanne. He tells of an embarrassing moment on stage when Fontanne's breast came out of her dress and later Lunt asked him, "Why didn't you put it back?" These days we call that a wardrobe malfunction.

Dick segued into the first-ever television sitcom, *I Remember Mama*, playing Peggy Wood's son Nels, a ratings winner for CBS in the newly-formed Nielsen ratings. When the show ended eight years later, Dick worked with Don Adams in *The Partners*, Jodi Foster in *Freaky Friday* and with his good friend Mel Brooks in *When Things Were Rotten* and *High Anxiety*, among others.

But Van Patten is best known for his lead role as the dad in *Eight Is Enough*, the popular comedy-drama series, and says, "In its five seasons, the show was always in the top ten and remains the highpoint of my career." He's held recurring roles in a series for six decades and starred in well over a hundred roles, including *The Love Boat*, *The Odd Couple*, *Happy Days*, and *Murder, She Wrote*, to name only a few. My late husband, screenwriter Gordon "Whitey" Mitchell, wrote and produced a pilot called *Rock Candy*, in which he starred.

Van Patten's wife Pat is a former June Taylor dancer. Their three sons

Dick shares a meal with his best friends.

are all actors, one named Nels after his role in *Mama*. His sister is actress Joyce Van Patten. Mel Brooks likes his humor so much he cast Dick in several of his movies. His close friend actress Susan Stafford says, "He's the most kind, loving and humorous man I know." Test his drollness out yourself: If you know his phone number, call it. If he's not there, after the greeting, you'll hear, "Remember the Chilean mine worker who had a mistress? Well, she was arrested for making love to a miner!" Or, if you ask the secret of his 57-year marriage, he'll tell you, "Weekly romantic candlelit dinners...she goes on Mondays, I go on Thursdays."

Over twenty years ago, Dick founded Natural Balance Pet Foods, which produces "the finest, healthiest pet food on the market," he boasts. It's not only for dogs and cats, but for lions, tigers and polar bears in zoos throughout the world and was on the pet menu at Michael Jackson's Neverland Ranch. It's sold at Petco and other independent stores. He supports the animal charities Guide Dogs of the Desert and the rescue organization ASPCA.

Dick Van Patten's book, *Eighty Is Not Enough: One Actor's Journey Through American Entertainment*, is filled with his wonderful anecdotes and can be found at Amazon.com. He's the proud owner of two stars, the other on the Hollywood Walk of Fame.

He's willing to share his star, too.

Adam West as Batman.

BAM! POW! ZONK!

ADAM WEST

STAR #329
DEDICATED APRIL 10, 2010
101 S. PALM CANYON DR.

BATMAN MAKES THE SCENE...that's the title of one of 120 episodes of the classic pop culture television series, *Batman*, Adam West starred in from 1966-68. He made the scene when the Walk of Stars honored him with a star.

A former drummer and singer, West always aimed to be an actor and received plenty of encouragement from his concert pianist-opera singer mom and later from his stepmom, who owned a theatre. In college, he sang and hosted a radio show and later, as a draftee, wrote sketches for the Army's first radio station. Years later, in Hawaii, a talent agent noticed West in a play and brought him to Hollywood where he landed theatrical roles in *The Young Philadelphians*, and many others. He guest-starred on the original *Outer Limits*, The Overland Trail and a number of other TV Westerns and, more recently, *30 Rock*.

"My agent sent me to Fox studios," West recalls, "to meet the producers of a new tongue-in-cheek series called *Batman*. I told him I'm trying to have a serious career here, and he said this is going to be big. I didn't even have to read for the role. They had seen me in a James Bond commercial and said, 'This is the guy that can play Batman!'" Adam is fond of saying he was part of the three Big B's of the 60s...Batman, The Beatles and Bond.

When *Batman* went out of production, Adam got busy doing personal appearances, guest shots, pilots, commercials, video games and voice-overs in several animated series such as *The Simpsons*, Nickelodeon's *The Fairly Odd Parents* and Fox network's *Family Guy*. All three are Emmy-winning shows. His appearance in movies, television series, specials, voice-overs, plays, radio shows, etc. totals over 160!

I asked how he felt about being typecast: "It's okay. This is the role the public holds dear. I'm the luckiest guy in the world. I had the opportunity

Adam West as himself.

not many actors get...to create an icon. I paid homage to the DC comic book character." (The first 1939 *Batman* comic book sold for a record-setting one million dollars!) Lee Meriwether, who played Catwoman in the 1966 *Batman* film, had this to say: "It's a joy to work with Adam West and listen to him tell his stories. He's brilliant at both comedy and dramatic roles." They are sometimes together for book and autograph signings events.

These days Adam West hikes, reads, swims, skis, enjoys fly-fishing, and spends time with Marcelle, his wife of forty-two years, and their blended family of six kids. "Besides, I've been asked to do another series," he adds. He's written his fascinating memoir, *Back to the Bat Cave*, which embraces the real story behind *Batman* and was made into a CBS TV movie. Batfans can purchase the book on his website at *adamwest.com*.

"I see stars," he quips, "walking on Palm Canyon Drive, I feel I've been around forever...I've worked with most of the stars I walk all over." Hundreds of fans tuned in on Bat-day, as the Caped Crusader received his own well-deserved Star. BAM! POW! ZONK!

Dan Westfall shares a moment with Cheeta.

MONKEY BUSINESS
DAN WESTFALL

STAR #332
DEDICATED OCTOBER 9, 2010
100 S. PALM CANYON DR.

Hailing originally from Ohio, Dan Westfall was always a dedicated show-business enthusiast and animal lover. He came to Hollywood in the early '60s and obtained his first entertainment industry job at ABC-TV as a page and a cue-card boy, working on numerous shows, including the *Lawrence Welk Show*, *The Hollywood Palace* and, much to his elation, The Academy Awards. Later, Dan worked with his uncle managing The Marquis Chimps, a trained animal act that appeared on The Jack Benny, Ed Sullivan and Dinah Shore shows and others.

Dan had been living with a chimp in a Los Angeles condo. In 1989, he checked with the city of Palm Springs and they advised him he'd be allowed to have exotic animals. Moving there, he found more suitable surroundings for his primate. "One night at a party," Dan recalls, "producer Riff Markowitz asked me if I'd be interested in joining the Palm Springs Follies." Dan and his chimps became the novelty act in the world-famous Follies. Later, Dan sang and danced in the chorus and was the comic relief in the show. His tenure at the *Follies* lasted a total of eleven seasons.

After promising to take good care of him, Dan inherited Cheeta from his uncle, animal trainer Tony Gentry. In the *Guinness Book of World's Records* as the oldest living non-human primate, Cheeta, who received his own star in 1995, mugged for the cameras in countless motion pictures and television shows. Cheeta's exact age seems in question. "I think he's in his seventies…or maybe it's the sixties," Dan says, uncertainly. "And it's a Hollywood mystery how many movies he's actually done. But Cheeta is the ambassador for all the chimps and other animals who've endured exploitation by the movie industry. They don't have to use these animals any longer now that they have sophisticated animatronics and digital technology."

Among Cheeta's talents is his artistic ability, which Dan wholly encourages. His artwork (Dan calls it "apestract art") has been displayed on the Regis Philbin and David Letterman shows and his paintings are exhibited in thirty countries worldwide. In proud possession of Cheeta's works are Larry King, Carol Channing, Ellen DeGeneres, Kaye Ballard and other celebrities.

At the encouragement of Dr. Jane Goodall, the renowned primatologist and anthropologist and world's foremost expert on chimpanzees, Westfall started the non-profit foundation The C.H.E.E.T.A. Primate Sanctuary, Inc., as a haven for ex-show business primates, which provides them with stimulating activities and a caring environment. He has donated two of Cheeta's paintings to the Goodall Institute which raised $20,000. On a recent visit to the sanctuary Dr. Goodall said, "This makes me feel that the world is still filled with people whose intents are wonderful and good." To contribute to the Cheeta Primate Sanctuary and receive a gift of "apestract" art, go to Cheetathechimp.org.

Dan Westfall and Cheeta will be together forever. At his wonderful ceremony, Dan's richly deserved star was placed…where else…? Right next to Cheeta's.

INDEX

A Star Is Born 13-15
Alexander, Bob 13-15, 167
Andrew, Dane 16-18
Asher, William 19-22

Bacino, Ted 23-27
Baker, Carroll 28-30
Ballard, Kaye 31-34
Barrett, Rona 35-38
Bole, Cliff 39-42

Caruso, Pattie Daly 43-46
Channing, Carol 47-52
Connors, Carol 53-56

Dante, Mary Jane 60
Dante, Michael 57-60
David, Kal & Lauri Bono 61-64
Dreesen, Tom 65-69

English, Joey 70-72
Evaro, Sonny & Family 73-76
Fleming, Rhonda 77-80

Gibson, Ruth 81-85
Greco, Buddy & Lezlie Anders 86-88
Greer, Gloria 89-92

Haber, Mel 93-96
Hall, Monty 97-100
Hay, Denise DuBarry 101-104
Hope, Bob 124, 192

Jeffries, Herb 105-109
Jones, Jack 110-112

Killijian, Harry 51-52
Kloss, Dorothy Dale 113-117

Lee, Ruta 118-121
Little, Rich 122-124
Lopez, Trini 125-129

Maltin, Anita 130-132
Marx, Barbara 136
Marx, Bill 133-136
Marx, Harpo 135-136
McGrath, Dan 137-141
McGrath, Regina 140
Mitchell, Gordon Whitey 88, 96, 128, 142-149, 160, 179, 204
Monroe, Marilyn 22, 200
Moody, Grace & Phil 150-152

New Christy Minstrels
 and Randy Sparks 153-157

Palm Springs Follies 117, 132, 211
Palm Springs Walk of Stars 13-15

Randall, Frankie 158-160
Read, Melinda 161-164
Reynolds, Debbie 165-168
Rizzo, Pat 160
Rubinsky, Irwin 132
Ruttan, Audrey 116

Shakespeare 26
Shores, Del 169-173
Sinatra, Barbara 174-177
Sinatra, Frank 22, 68, 92, 127,
 159-160, 178-180, 184, 195
Smith, Keely 181-184
Stafford, Susan 185-189
Stevens, Connie 190-192

Vale, Jerry 193-196
Van Doren, Mamie 197-200
Van Patten, Dick 201-205

West, Adam 206-209
Westfall, Dan 210-212

Bear Manor Media

Classic Cinema.
Timeless TV.
Retro Radio.

WWW.BEARMANORMEDIA.COM

www.ingramcontent.com/pod-product-compliance
Lightning Source LLC
Chambersburg PA
CBHW070740160426
43192CB00009B/1509